Ho Chi Minh City & Mekong Delta

Claire Boobbyer

Credits

Footprint credits

Editor: Alan Murphy
Production and layout: Angus Dawson, Emma Bryers
Maps: Kevin Feeney

Managing Director: Andy Riddle
Commercial Director: Patrick Dawson
Publisher: Alan Murphy
Publishing Managers: Felicity Laughton, Nicola Gibbs.
Digital Editors: Jo Williams, Tom Mellors
Marketing and PR: Liz Harper
Sales: Diane McEntee
Advertising: Renu Sibal
Finance and Administration: Elizabeth Taylor

Photography credits

Front cover: Bzzuspajk/Shutterstock
Back cover: Luciano Mortula/Shutterstock

Printed in Great Britain by CPI Antony Rowe, Chippenham, Wiltshire

Every effort has been made to ensure that the facts in this guidebook are accurate. However, travellers should still obtain advice from consulates, airlines, etc about travel and visa requirements before travelling. The authors and publishers cannot accept responsibility for any loss, injury or inconvenience however caused.

Publishing information

Footprint *Focus Ho Chi Minh City & Mekong Delta*
1st edition
© Footprint Handbooks Ltd
July 2011

ISBN: 978 1 908206 08 4
CIP DATA: A catalogue record for this book is available from the British Library

® Footprint Handbooks and the Footprint mark are a registered trademark of Footprint Handbooks Ltd

Published by Footprint
6 Riverside Court
Lower Bristol Road
Bath BA2 3DZ, UK
T +44 (0)1225 469141
F +44 (0)1225 469461
footprinttravelguides.com

Distributed in the USA by Globe Pequot Press, Guilford, Connecticut

The content of Footprint *Focus Ho Chi Minh City & the Mekong Delta* has been taken directly from Footprint's *Vietnam Handbook* which was researched and written by Claire Boobbyer.

Contents

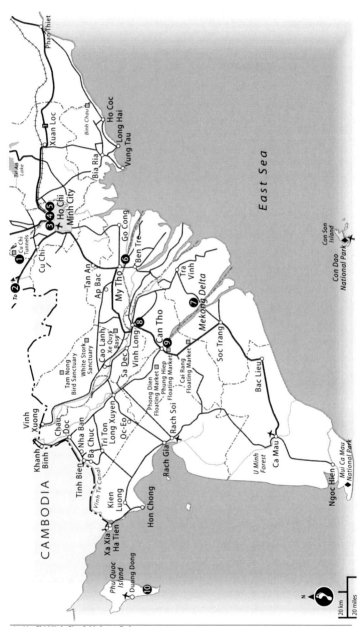

CAMBODIA

East Sea

Phan Thiet
Xuan Loc
Ho Coc
Long Hai
Vung Tau
Bia Ria
Binh Chau
Tri An Lake
3·4·5 Ho Chi Minh City
1 Cu Chi Tunnels
Cu Chi
To **2**
Tan An
Ap Bac
Go Cong
6 My Tho
Ben Tre
Tra Vinh
7
Cao Lanh
Ye Quyt Bass
Sa Dec
Vinh Long
8 Can Tho
9
Mekong Delta
Soc Trang
Phong Dien Floating Market
Phung Hiep Floating Market
Cai Rang Floating Market
White Stork Sanctuary
Tam Nong Bird Sanctuary
Vinh Xuong
Khanh Binh
Chau Doc
Nha Ban
Ba Chuc
Tinh Bien
Tri Ton
Long Xuyen
Oc-Eo
Rach Soi
Rach Gia
Bac Lieu
Vinh Te Canal
Kien Luong
Hon Chong
Xa Xia
Ha Tien
Duong Dong
Phu Quoc Island
U Minh Forest
Ca Mau
Ngoc Hien
Mui Ca Mau National Park
Con Son Island
Con Dao National Park
10

N

20 km
20 miles

4 ● Ho Chi Minh City & Mekong Delta

Ho Chi Minh City, Pearl of the Orient, is the largest and most dynamic city in one of the most rapidly growing economies in the world. Founded as a Khmer trading and fishing port on the west bank of the Dong Nai River, it was destroyed by French naval forces in 1859, then rebuilt as a French colonial city and named Saigon (*Soai-gon* – 'wood of the kapok tree'), capital of French Cochin China. During the 1960s and early 1970s Saigon boomed and flourished under the American occupation and was the seat of the South Vietnam government until liberation (or fall, depending upon your point of view). Officially Ho Chi Minh City (HCMC) since 1975, it remains to most the bi-syllabic, familiar, old 'Saigon'.

Today Ho Chi Minh City is a place of remorseless and relentless activity. Despite government restrictions thousands of young men and women make their way here every week in search of a better life. They come in droves to work, study, meet, marry and live. The city is growing at a prodigious rate: 25 years ago Tan Son Nhat, the airport, was right out at the edge of the city; it has been an inner suburb for years, long ago leapfrogged by the sprawl that is pushing outwards into former paddy fields with astonishing speed.

Formal sights are thin on the ground in the Mekong Delta, the rice basket of Vietnam, and travel can be slow, involving ferry crossings and boat rides although year on year new bridges are being built linking hitherto remote islands to main lines of communication. But herein lies the first contradiction of the delta, for the journey is often more fun than the destination. Boat trips along canals, down rivers and around islands hold more appeal than many of the towns and the main roads that are straggled with mile upon mile of homes and small industry. Driving past paddy fields or cycling through orchards is often more enchanting than the official tourist stops.

Planning your trip

When to go

Climatically the best time to see Vietnam is around December to March when it should be dry and not too hot. In the south it is warm but not too hot with lovely cool evenings. Admittedly the north and the highlands will be a bit chilly but they should be dry with clear blue skies. The tourist industry high season is normally November to May when hotel prices tend to rise and booking flights can be hard. Travel in the south and Mekong Delta can be difficult at the height of the monsoon (particularly September, October and November). The central regions and north sometimes suffer typhoons and tropical storms from May to November. Hué is at its wettest from September to January.

Despite its historic and cultural resonance Tet, or Vietnamese New Year, is not a good time to visit. This movable feast usually falls between late January and March and, with aftershocks, lasts for about a fortnight. It is the only holiday most people get in the year. Popular destinations are packed, roads are jammed and for a couple of days almost all restaurants are shut. All hotel prices increase, and car hire prices are increased by 50% or more. The best prices are from May to October.

During the school summer holidays some resorts get busy. At Cat Ba, Sapa, Phan Thiet, Long Hai and Phu Quoc, for example, prices rise, there is a severe squeeze on rooms and weekends are worse. The Central Highlands tend to fare much better with cool temperatures and a good availability of rooms.

Getting there

Air

Vietnam is relatively isolated in comparison with Bangkok, Hong Kong and Singapore. Most major airlines have direct flights from Europe, North America and Australasia to these hubs. Ho Chi Minh City, and to a lesser extent Hanoi, is pretty well connected with other Southeast Asian countries which remain the source of most foreign visitors. Connections have also increased in the last few years with the rise of budget airlines. Prices vary according to high (November to April, July and August) and low season.

Flights from Europe In Western Europe, there are direct flights to Vietnam from Paris and Frankfurt with **Vietnam Airlines/Air France**. These code-shared flights last 12 hours. **Vietnam Airlines** has an office in the UK or book flights online. There are also direct **Vietnam Airlines** flights from Moscow.

Flights from London and other European hubs go via Bangkok, Singapore, Kuala Lumpur, Hong Kong or UAE states. From London to Vietnam, flights take 16 to 18 hours, depending on the length of stopover. Airlines include **Air France**, **Cathay Pacific**, **Emirates**, **Gulf Air**, **Thai International**, **Singapore Airlines**, **Malaysia Airlines**, **Lufthansa**, and **Qatar**. It is possible to fly into Hanoi and depart from Ho Chi Minh City although this does seem to rack up the return fare. Check details with flight agents and tour operators (see pages 12 and 23).

Flights from the USA and Canada By far the best option is to fly via **Bangkok**, **Taipei**, **Tokyo** or **Hong Kong** and from there to Vietnam. The approximate flight time from Los Angeles to **Bangkok** is 21 hours. **United** flies from LA and Chicago via Tokyo and from San

Don't miss ...

Numbers relate to numbers on map on page 4.

Francisco via Seoul to Vietnam. **Thai**, **Delta**, **United** and **Air Canada** fly to Bangkok from a number of US and Canadian cities.

Flights from Australia and New Zealand There are direct flights from Adelaide, Melbourne, Sydney, Perth, Auckland and Wellington with **Cathay Pacific**, **Malaysia Airlines**, **Singapore Airlines** and **Thai**. **Qantas** flies from Sydney, Adelaide and Melbourne to Ho Chi Minh City.

Budget airlines from Australia include **Jetstar** and **Tiger Airways**. From Sydney the flights to Vietnam are eight hours 45 minutes direct.

Flights from Asia

Thai flies from Bangkok to Ho Chi Minh City and Hanoi. **AirAsia** flies from Bangkok and Kuala Lumpur to Ho Chi Minh City and from Kuala Lumpur and Bangkok to Hanoi. **Vietnam Airlines** flies from Bangkok, Phnom Penh, Siem Reap, Vientiane, Luang Prabang, Beijing, Guangzhou, Kunming, Hong Kong, Kuala Lumpur, Singapore, Manila, Busan, Seoul, Japan and Taipei. **Laos Airlines** flies from Luang Prabang and Vientiane. **Malaysia Airlines** flies from Kuala Lumpur to Hanoi and Ho Chi Minh City. **Tiger Airways** flies from Singapore to Ho Chi Minh City and Hanoi. **Cathay Pacific** flies from Hong Kong. **China Airlines** flies from Taipei to Ho Chi Minh City. **Japan Airlines** flies from Tokyo to Ho Chi Minh City and Hanoi. **Korean Air** flies from Seoul to Ho Chi Minh City and Hanoi. **Philippine Airlines** flies from Manila to Ho Chi Minh City. **Singapore Airlines** flies to Hanoi and Ho Chi Minh City. **Thai International** flies from Bangkok to Ho Chi Minh City and from Sydney and Melbourne to Ho Chi Minh City and Hanoi.

Airport information

There are two main international airports in Vietnam: **Tan Son Nhat Airport** (SGN) in Ho Chi Minh City, and **Noi Bai Airport** (HAN) in Hanoi. **Danang** (DAD), has a couple of international flights.

Getting around

Air

Vietnam Airlines is the national carrier and flies to multiple domestic destinations. **Vietnam Airlines** changes its schedule every six months so check before making any plans.

Refunds, rebookings and rerouting may not be allowed on certain ticket fares. Remember that during holiday periods flights get extremely busy.

Rail

Train travel is exciting and overnight journeys are a good way of covering long distances. The Vietnamese rail network extends from Hanoi to Ho Chi Minh City. **Vietnam Railways** (www.vr.com.vn) runs the 2600-km rail network down the coast. With overnight stays at hotels along the way to see the sights, a rail sightseeing tour from Hanoi to Ho Chi Minh City should take a minimum of 10 days but you would need to buy tickets for each separate section of the journey.

The difference in price between first and second class is small and it is worth paying the extra. There are three seating classes and four sleeping classes including hard and soft seats and hard and soft sleepers; some are air-conditioned, others are not. The prices vary according to the class of cabin and the berth chosen; the bottom berth is more expensive than the top berth. All sleepers should be booked three days in advance. The kitchen on the Hanoi to Ho Chi Minh City service serves soups and simple, but adequate, rice dishes (it is a good idea to take additional food and drink on long journeys). First-class long-distance tickets include the price of meals. The express trains (**Reunification Express**) take between an advertised 29½ to 34 hours; odd-numbered trains travel from Hanoi to Ho Chi Minh City, even-numbered trains vice versa.

Most ticket offices have some staff who speak English. Queues can be long and some offices keep unusual hours. If you are short of time and short on patience it may well pay to get a tour operator to book your ticket for a small commission or visit the Ho Chi Minh City railway office in Pham Ngu Lao or the Hanoi agency in the Old Quarter.

There are also rail routes from Hanoi to Haiphong, to Lang Son and to Lao Cai. The **Victoria** hotel chain (www.victoriahotels-asia.com) runs a luxury carriage on the latter route.

River

In the south, there are services from Chau Doc to Phnom Penh. The **Victoria** hotel chain (www.victoriahotels-asia.com) runs a Mekong Delta service for its guests. Ferries operate between Ho Chi Minh City and Vung Tau; Rach Gia and Phu Quoc; Ha Tien and Phu Quoc; Haiphong and Cat Ba Island; and Halong City and Cat Ba and Mong Cai.

Road

Open Tour Buses, see below, are very useful and cheap for bridging important towns. Many travellers opt to take a tour to reach remote areas because of the lack of self-drive car hire and the dangers and slow speed of public transport.

Bus Roads in Vietnam are notoriously dangerous. As American humourist PJ O'Rourke wrote: "In Japan people drive on the left. In China people drive on the right. In Vietnam it doesn't matter." Since Highway 1 is so dangerous and public transport buses are poor and slow, most travellers opt for the cheap and regular **Open Tour Bus** (private minibus or coach) that covers the length of the country. Almost every Vietnamese tour operator/ travellers' café listed in this guide will run a minibus service or act as an agent. The ticket is a flexible, one-way ticket from Ho Chi Minh City to Hanoi and vice versa, see box page 23. The buses run daily from their own offices and include the following stops: Ho Chi Minh City, Mui Ne, Nha Trang, Dalat, Hoi An, Hué, Ninh Binh and Hanoi. They will also stop off at tourist destinations along the way such as Lang Co, Hai Van Pass, Marble Mountains and Po Klong Garai for quick visits. You may join at any leg of the journey, paying for one trip or several as you go. The Hanoi to Hué and vice versa is an overnight trip but although you might save on a night's accommodation you are unlikely to get much sleep.

If you do opt for **public buses** note that most bus stations are on the outskirts of town; in bigger centres there may be several stations. Long-distance buses invariably leave very early in the morning (0400-0500). Buses are the cheapest form of transport, although sometimes foreigners find they are being asked for two to three times the correct price. Prices are normally prominently displayed at bus stations. It helps if you can find out what the correct fare should be in advance. Less comfortable but quicker are the minibus services, which ply the more popular routes.

Car hire Self-drive car hire is not available in Vietnam. It is, however, possible to hire cars with drivers and this is a good way of getting to more remote areas with a group of people. Cars with drivers can be hired for around US$60-110 per day. Longer trips would see a reduced cost. All cars are air-conditioned. Car hire prices increase by 50% or more during Tet.

Motorbike and bicycle hire Most towns are small enough to get around by bicycle, and this can also be a pleasant way to explore the surrounding countryside. However, if covering large areas (touring around the Central Highlands, for example) then a motorbike will mean you can see more and get further off the beaten track.

Motorbikes and bicycles can be hired by the day in the cities, often from hotels and travellers' cafés. You do not need a driver's licence or proof of motorbike training to hire a motorbike in Vietnam, however, it became compulsory in 2007 to wear a helmet. Take time to familiarize yourself with road conditions and ride slowly. Motorbikes cost around US$6 per day including helmet; bicycles can be hired for US$1-2 including a lock. Always park your bicycle or motorbike in a gui xe (guarded parking place) and ask for a ticket. The small cost is worth every dong, even if you are just popping into the post office to post a letter.

Motorbike taxi and cyclo Motorcycle taxis, known as *honda ôm* or *xe ôm* (*ôm* means to cuddle) are ubiquitous and cheap. You will find them on most street corners, outside hotels or in the street. With their baseball caps and dangling cigarette, *xe ôm* drivers are readily recognizable. If they see you before you see them, they will shout 'moto' to get your attention. In the north and upland areas the Honda is replaced with the Minsk. The shortest hop would be at least 10,000d. Always bargain though.

Cyclos are bicycle trishaws. Cyclo drivers charge double or more that of a *xe ôm*. A number of streets in the centres of Ho Chi Minh City and Hanoi are one-way or out of bounds to cyclos, necessitating lengthy detours which add to the time and cost. Do not take a cyclo after dark unless the driver is well known to you or you know the route. It is a wonderful way to get around the Old Quarter of Hanoi, though, and for those with plenty of time on their hands it is not as hazardous in smaller towns.

Taxi Taxis ply the streets of Hanoi and Ho Chi Minh City and other large towns and cities. They are cheap, around 12,000d per kilometre, and the drivers are better English speakers than cyclo drivers. Always keep a small selection of small denomination notes with you so that when the taxi stops you can round up the fare to the nearest small denomination. At night use the better known taxi companies rather than the unlicensed cars that often gather around popular nightspots.

Sleeping

Accommodation ranges from luxury suites in international five-star hotels and spa resorts to small, family hotels (mini hotels) and homestays with local people in the Mekong Delta and with the ethnic minorities in the Central Highlands and northern Vietnam. During peak seasons – especially December to March and particularly during busy holidays such as Tet, Christmas, New Year's Eve and around Easter – booking is essential. Expect staff to speak English in all top hotels. Do not expect it in cheaper hotels or in more remote places, although most places employ someone with a smattering of a foreign language.

Private, mini hotels are worth seeking out as, being family-run, guests can expect good service. Mid-range and tourist hotels may provide a decent breakfast which is often included in the price. Many luxury and first-class hotels and some three-star hotels charge extra for breakfast and, on top of this, also charge 10% VAT and 5% service charge. When quoted a hotel price you should ask whether that includes these two taxes; it is marked as ++ (plus plus) on the bill.

There are some world-class beach resorts in Phu Quoc, Nha Trang, Mui Ne, Hoi An and Danang. In the northern uplands, in places like Sapa, Ha Giang province and Mai Chau, it is possible to stay in an ethnic minority house. Bathrooms are basic and will consist of a cold shower or warm shower and a natural or western toilet. To stay in a homestay, you must book through a tour operator or through the local tourist office; you cannot just turn up. Homestays are also possible on farms and in orchards in the Mekong Delta. Guests sleep on camp beds and share a Western bathroom. National parks offer everything from air-conditioned bungalows to shared dormitory rooms to campsites where, sometimes, it is possible to hire tents. Visitors may spend a romantic night on a boat in Halong Bay or on the Mekong Delta. Boats range from the fairly luxurious to the basic. Most people book through tour operators. In remote places where there is no competition, dour and surly service remain the order of the day. **The Vietnam Hostelling International Association** (www.hihostels.com) has been established, operating hostels in Hanoi, Hoi An and Sapa.

You will have to leave your passport at hotel reception desks for the duration of your hotel stay. It will be released to you temporarily for bank purposes or buying an air ticket. Credit cards are widely accepted but there is often a 2-4% fee for paying in this manner. Tipping is not expected in hotels in Vietnam.

Camping in Vietnam is limited mainly because the authorities insist on foreign visitors sleeping in registered accommodation. There are no campsites but visitors bringing tents may be able to use them around Sapa or on Cat Ba and surrounding islands. Some guesthouses in Mui Ne and other seaside places have tents.

If you wish to stay at the **house of a friend** this is normally permitted but your hosts will need to take your passport and arrival form to their local police station. Police and People's Committee regulations in some towns mean that a foreigner travelling with his Vietnamese wife must bring a marriage certificate in order to share a hotel room with her.

The age of consent in Vietnam is 18. There are rules relating to a Vietnamese person of the opposite sex being in your hotel room. It depends on the attitude of the hotel. If the Vietnamese person is your partner, as opposed to a one-night stand, hotels are more relaxed. However, Hoi An is the exception and you will have to rent a second room. This is also the policy in international hotels in big cities, not because international chains have moral qualms but because they get penalized by the police. Local hotels from which the police can collect bribes tend to be more 'accommodating'.

Sleeping and eating price codes

Sleeping

$$$$ over US$100	$$$ US$46-100	$$ US$20-45
$ under US$20		

Prices include taxes and service charge, but not meals. They are based on a double room, except in the $ range, where prices are almost always per person.

Eating

¶¶¶ over US$12	¶¶ US$6-12	¶ under US$6

Prices refer to the cost of a two-course meal for one person, excluding drinks or service charge.

Travellers normally get their laundry done in hotels. In cheap hotels it's inexpensive. Cheaper hotels and laundries in the hotel districts charge by weight. The smarter places charge by the item and the bill can be a shock! Always check bills; overcharging is common.

Eating and drinking

Food

Food is a major attraction of Vietnam and it is one of the paradoxes of this enigmatic country that so much food should be so readily and deliciously available. Eating out is so cheap that practically every meal eaten by the visitor will be taken in a restaurant or café. Ho Chi Minh City and Hanoi offer a wide range of cuisines besides Vietnamese, so that only Congolese, Icelandic and English tourists will be deprived of home cooking.

Vietnam offers outstanding Vietnamese, French and international cuisine in restaurants that range from first class to humble foodstalls. The quality will be, in the main, exceptional. The accent is on local, seasonal and fresh produce and the rich pickings from the sea, along Vietnam's 2000-km coastline will always make it far inland too. You will find more hearty stews in the more remote north and more salad dishes along the coast. All restaurants offer a variety of cuisine from the regions and some specialize in certain types of food – Hué cuisine, Cha Ca Hanoi, etc. *Pho* (pronounced *fer*), a bowl of flat, white, noodle soup served with chicken or beef, is utterly delicious. The soup is made from stock flavoured with star anise, ginger and other spices and herbs but individual recipes often remain a closely guarded secret. Vietnamese usually eat *pho* in the morning, often in the evening but rarely at lunchtime, when they require a more filling meal accompanied by rice. On each table of a *pho* restaurant sits a plate of fresh green leaves: mint, cinnamon, basil and the spiky looking *ngo gai*, together with bean sprouts, chopped red chillies, barbecue sauce and sliced lemons, enabling patrons to produce their own variations on a theme.

Another local speciality which visitors often overlook is *com tam* or broken rice. *Com tam* stalls abound on the streets and do brisk trade at breakfast and lunch. They tend to be low-cost canteens, but in many cities they have appeal to the wealthier office market and have started to abandon tiny plastic stools in favour of proper tables and chairs and concentrate more on cleanliness and presentation. The steamed broken rice is eaten with fried chicken, fish, pork and vegetables and soup is normally included in the price.

There are many types of Vietnamese roll: the most common are deep-fried spring rolls (confusingly, *cha gio* in the south and *nem ranh* in the north) but if these appear on your table too frequently, look for the fresh or do-it-yourself types, such as *bi cuon* or *bo bia*. Essentially, these are salads with prawns or grilled meats wrapped in rice paper. Customers who roll their own cigarettes are at a distinct advantage while innocents abroad are liable to produce sagging Camberwell Carrots that collapse in the lap.

Vietnamese salads (*goi* in the south and *nom* in the north) are to die for. The best known is the green papaya salad with dried beef (*nom du du bo kho*); others include *goi xoai* (mango salad) and *goi buoi* (pomelo salad). They all involve a wonderful fusion of herbs and vegetables with sweet and spicy tastes rolled in.

Delicious seafood is a staple across the land. It would be invidious to isolate a particular seafood dish when there are so many to chose from. Prawns are prawns – the bigger and the less adulterated the better. But a marvellous dish that does deserve commendation is crab in tamarind sauce. This glorious fusion of flavours, bitter tamarind, garlic, piquant spring onion and fresh crab is quite delicious. To the Vietnamese, part of the fun of eating crab is the fiddly process of extracting meat from the furthest recesses of its claws and legs. A willingness to crack, crunch, poke and suck is required to do it justice, not a task for the squeamish but great for those who aren't.

All Vietnamese food is dipped, whether in fish sauce, soy sauce, chilli sauce, peanut sauce or pungent prawn sauce (*mam tom* – avoid if possible) before eating. As each course is served so a new set of dips will accompany. Follow the guidance of your waiter or Vietnamese friends to get the right dip with the right dish.

When it comes to food, Vietnamese do not stand on ceremony and (perhaps rather like the French) regard peripherals such as furniture, service and ambience as mere distractions to the task of ploughing through plates, crocks, casseroles and tureens charged with piping hot meats, vegetables and soups. Do not expect good service, courses to arrive in the right order, or to eat at the same time as your companions, but do expect the freshest and tastiest food you will find anywhere.

While it is possible to eat very cheaply in Vietnam (especially outside Hanoi and Ho Chi Minh City) the higher class of restaurant, particularly those serving foreign cuisine, can prove quite expensive, especially with wine. But with judicious shopping around it is not hard to find excellent value for money, particularly in the small, **family restaurants**. In the listing sections we describe a range of diners which should satisfy every palate and every pocket and in the Hanoi chapter we provide information on street stalls. Some restaurants (mostly expensive ones) add 5% service charge and the government tax of 10% to the bill. See box, page 11 on restaurant classification.

For day trips, an early morning visit to the **markets** will produce a picnic fit for a king. Hard-boiled quails' eggs, thinly sliced garlic sausage and salami, pickled vegetables, beef tomatoes, cucumber, pâté, cheese, warm baguettes and fresh fruit. And, far from costing a king's ransom, it will feed four for around US$1 a head.

The thing that separates India from China is that in the former there are prohibitions governing the consumption of just about everything. In the latter anything and everything can be – and is – eaten. Vietnam of course falls under Chinese sway. Therefore anyone who self imposes restrictions on his eating habits is regarded as a bit of a crank. There are **vegetarian restaurants** in Vietnam but these usually sell different types of tofu dressed to look like meat. The vegetable section of most 'normal' restaurants has vegetables – but cooked with pork, with beef or with prawns, rarely pure vegetables. Nevertheless there are a few Vietnamese vegetarians and twice a month a great many people eat vegetarian so restaurants are aware of the concept. We have listed for most bigger towns some highly acclaimed vegetarian restaurants and places on the backpacker trail that are on the ball.

Given the large proportion of the population aged 16 and under no Vietnamese restaurant is put out by **children**. Indeed any restaurant frequented by Vietnamese families will have kids running around everywhere. So parents need have no fears about their children's behaviour upsetting anyone. Obviously in smarter places unruly children may not be so popular so beware invitations to 'take a tour of the kitchen'.

Note that Vietnamese get up early and so lunch time starts at 1100 although restaurants catering for foreigners stay open until 1400, but don't leave lunch later than that as many places close the kitchen until the dinner trade at around 1700.

Drink

Locally produced fresh beer is called *bia hoi*. It is cold and refreshing, and weak and cheap enough to drink in quite large volumes. It is usually consumed in small pavement cafés where patrons sit on small plastic stools. Most *bia hoi* cafés serve simple and inexpensive food. Almost all customers are men and they can get a bit jolly. As the beer is fresh it has to be consumed within a short period of brewing hence most towns, even quite small ones, have their own brewery and impart to their beer a local flavour in a way that used to happen in England before the big brewers took over. Unfortunately bars and restaurants do not sell *bia hoi* as it's too cheap, at just 4000d per litre. Hence bar customers have a choice of Tiger, Heineken, Carlsberg, San Miguel, 333, Saigon Beer or Huda. All are brewed in Vietnam but many visitors try to stick to the local beers (333, Saigon and Huda) as they are cheaper and, to many, more distinctively flavoursome than the mass produced international brands. Unfortunately this is not always possible as many bars and restaurants stock only the more expensive beers of the big international brewers because they have higher mark-ups.

Rice and **fruit wines** are produced and consumed in large quantities in upland areas, particularly in the north of Vietnam. Rice wines are fairly easily found, however. There are two types of rice wine, *ruou nep* and *ruou de*. *Ruou nep* is a viscous wine made from sticky rice. It is purple and white due to the different types of rice used to make it. Among the ethnic minorities, who are recognized as masters of rice wine, *ruou nep* is drunk from a ceramic jar through a straw. This communal drinking is an integral part of their way of life and no doubt contributes substantially to strengthening the ties of the clan. It is possible to become very drunk drinking *ruou nep* without realizing it. *Ruou de* is a rice spirit and very strong.

The Chinese believe that **snake wines** increase their virility and are normally found in areas with a large Chinese population. It is called a wine despite being a spirit. Other wines include the body and parts of seahorses, gecko, silkworms and bees.

There is a fantastic range of different **fruit wines** but unless you make a real effort it can be quite hard to find them. Wines are made from just about all upland fruits: plum, strawberry, apple and, of course, grapes, although grape wine in Vietnam is generally disappointing. The others are fiery and warm, strong and, bought by the bottle, cheap.

Responsible tourism and cultural sensitivities

Vietnam is remarkably relaxed and easy going with regard to conventions. The people, especially in small towns and rural areas, can be pretty old-fashioned, but it is difficult to cause offence unwittingly. The main complaint Vietnamese have of foreigners is their fondness for dirty and torn clothing. Backpackers come in for particularly severe criticism and the term *tay ba lo* (literally 'Western backpacker') is a contemptuous one reflecting the low priority many budget travellers seem to allocate to personal hygiene and the antiquity and inadequacy of their shorts and vests.

Shoes should be removed before entering temples and before going into people's houses. Modesty should be preserved and excessive displays of bare flesh are not considered good form, particularly in temples and private houses. (Not that the Vietnamese are unduly prudish, they just like things to be kept in their proper place.) Shorts are fine for the beach and travellers' cafés but not for smart restaurants.

Kissing and canoodling in public are likely to draw attention, not much of it favourable. But walking hand in hand is now accepted as a Western habit. Hand shaking among men is a standard greeting and although Vietnamese women will consent to the process, it is often clear that they would prefer not to. The head is held by some to be sacred and people would rather you didn't pat them on it. The Vietnamese do not share the concern about having someone's feet higher than their head.

Terms of address

Vietnamese names are written with the surname first, followed by the first name. Thus Nguyen Minh is not called Nguyen as we would presume in the West but Minh. In addressing people who are the same age as you but who you don't know, you would call them *anh* (for a man) and *chi* (for a woman). When you know their first name you would say 'anh Minh', for example.

Essentials A-Z

Accident and emergency
Contact the relevant emergency service and your embassy. Make sure you obtain police/medical records in order to file insurance claims. If you need to report a crime, visit your local police station and take a local with you who speaks English.
Ambulance T115, **Fire** T114, **Police** T113.

Disabled travellers
Considering the proportion of the country's population that is seriously disabled, foreigners might expect better facilities and allowances for the immobile. But there are very few. However, some of the more upmarket hotels do have a few designated rooms for the disabled. For those with walking difficulties many of the better hotels do have lifts. Wheelchair access is improving with more shopping centres, hotels and restaurants providing ramps for easy access. People sensitive to noise will find Vietnam, at times, almost intolerable.
RADAR, 12 City Forum, 250 City Rd, London, EC1V 8AF, T020-7250 3222, www.radar.org.uk.
SATH, 347 Fifth Av, Suite 605, New York City, NY 10016, T212-447 7284, www.sath.org.

Electricity
Voltage 110-240. Sockets are round 2-pin. Sometimes they are 2 flat pin. A number of top hotels now use UK 3 square-pin sockets.

Embassies and consulates
Australia, 6 Timbarra Cres, O'Malley Canberra, ACT 2606, T+61-2 6286 6059, www.vietnamembassy.org.au.
Cambodia, 436 Monivong, Phnom Penh, T+855 23-726274, www.vietnamembassy-cambodia.org.
Canada, 470 Wilbrod St, Ottawa, Ontario, K1N 6M8, T+1 613-236 0772, www.vietnamembassy-canada.ca.

China, 32 Guanghua R, Jiangou menwai, PO Box 00600, Beijing, T+86-10 6532 1155; 5/F, Great Smart Tower, 230 Van Chai Rd, Wan Chai, Hong Kong, T852-2591 4517, http://www.vnemba.org.cn/en.
France, 62 R Boileau-75016, Paris, T+33 144-146400, www.vietnamembassy-france.org/en.
Laos, 85 23 Singha Rd, Vientiane, T+856 21-413409, www.mofa.gov.vn/vnemb.la.
South Africa, 87 Brooks St, Brooklyn, Pretoria, T+27 12-362 8119, www.vietnamembassy-southafrica.org/en/.
Thailand, 83/1 Wireless Rd, Lumpini, Pathumwan, Bangkok 10330, T+66 2-251 5837, www.vietnamembassy-thailand.org/en.
UK, 12-14 Victoria Rd, London W8 5RD, T+44 (0)20-7937 1912, www.vietnamembassy.org.uk/consular.html.
USA, 1233, 20th St, NW Suite 400 Washington DC, 20036, T+1 202 861 0737, www.vietnamembassy-usa.org.

Health
See your doctor or travel clinic at least 6 weeks before your departure for general advice on travel risks, malaria and vaccinations (see also below). Make sure you have travel insurance, get a dental check-up (especially if you are going to be away for more than a month), know your own blood group and if you suffer a long-term condition such as diabetes or epilepsy make sure someone knows or that you have a **Medic Alert** bracelet/necklace with this information on it (www.medicalert.co.uk).

Health risks
Malaria exists in rural areas in Vietnam. However, there is no risk in the Red River Delta and the coastal plains north of Nha Trang. Neither is there a risk in Hanoi, HCMC, Danang and Nha Trang. The choice

of malaria prophylaxis will need to be something other than chloroquine for most people, since there is such a high level of resistance to it. Always check with your doctor or travel clinic for the most up-to-date advice.

Malaria can cause death within 24 hrs. It can start as something just resembling an attack of flu. You may feel tired, lethargic, headachy, feverish; or more seriously, develop fits, followed by coma and then death. Have a low index of suspicion because it is very easy to write off vague symptoms, which may actually be malaria. If you have a temperature, go to a doctor as soon as you can and ask for a malaria test. On your return home if you suffer any of these symptoms, get tested as soon as possible, even if any previous test proved negative; the test could save your life.

The most serious viral disease is **dengue fever**, which is hard to protect against as the mosquitos bite throughout the day as well as at night. Bacterial diseases include **tuberculosis** (TB) and some causes of the more common traveller's **diarrhoea**. Lung fluke (**para-gonimiasis**) occurs in Vietnam. A fluke is a sort of flattened worm. In the Sin Ho district the locals like to eat undercooked or raw crabs, but our advice is to leave them to it. The crabs contain a fluke which, when eaten, travels to the lungs. The lung fluke may cause a cough, coughing 'blood', fever, chest pain and changes on your X-ray which will puzzle a British radiologist. The cure is the same drug that cures schistosomiasis (another fluke which can be acquired in some parts of the Mekong delta).

Each year there is the possibility that **avian flu** or **SARS** may again rear their ugly heads. Check the news reports. If there is a problem in an area you are due to visit you may be advised to have an ordinary flu shot or to seek expert advice. Vietnam has had a number of fatalities from Avian influenza. Consult the WHO website, www. who.int, for further information and heed local advice on the ground. There are high rates of **HIV** in the region, especially among sex workers. See also box, page 11.

Medical services
Western hospitals staffed by foreign and Vietnamese medics exist in Hanoi and HCMC. See under medical services in each area for listings.

Useful websites
www.btha.org British Travel Health Association (UK). This is the official website of an organization of travel health professionals. **www.cdc.gov** US government site that gives excellent advice on travel health and details of disease outbreaks. **www.fitfortravel.scot.nhs.uk** A-Z of vaccine/health advice for each country. **www.who.int** The WHO *Blue Book* lists the diseases of the world.

Vaccinations
The following vaccinations are advised: BCG, Hepatitis A, Japanese Encephalitis, Polio, Rabies, Tetanus, Typhoid and Yellow Fever.

Insurance
Always take out travel insurance before you set off and read the small print carefully. Check that the policy covers the activities you intend or may end up doing. Also check exactly what your medical cover includes, such as ambulance, helicopter rescue or emergency flights back home. Also check the payment protocol. You may have to pay up first before the insurance company reimburses you. Keep receipts for expensive personal effects, such as jewellery or cameras. Take photos of these items and note down all serial numbers. You are advised to shop around. **STA Travel** and other reputable student travel organizations offer good value policies. Companies like **BUPA** offer good and comprehensive cover. Young travellers from North America can try the **International Student Insurance Service** (ISIS), which is available through **STA Travel**, T1-800-781-4040, www.sta-travel.

com. Other recommended companies in North America include: **Access America**, www.accessamerica.com; **Travel Insurance Services**, www.travelinsure.com; and **Travel Assistance International**, www.travel assistance.com. Older travellers should note that some companies will not cover people over 65 years old, or may charge higher premiums. The best policies for older travellers in the UK are offered by **Age UK**, www.ageuk.org.uk.

Language
You are likely to find some English spoken wherever there are tourist services but outside tourist centres communication can be a problem for those who have no knowledge of Vietnamese. Furthermore, the Vietnamese language is not easy to learn. For example, pronunciation presents enormous difficulties as it is tonal: it has 6 tones, 12 vowels and 27 consonants. On the plus side, Vietnamese is written in a Roman alphabet making life much easier; place and street names are instantly recognizable. French is still spoken and often very well by the more elderly and educated Vietnamese.

In HCMC, language courses of several months' duration are offered by various organizations. In Hanoi, contact www.hiddenhanoi.com.vn.

Money → US$1 = 20,584, £1 = 33,875, €1 = 29,457 (May 2011)
The unit of currency is the dong. Under law, shops should only accept dong but in practice this is not enforced and dollars are accepted almost everywhere. If possible, however, try to pay for everything in dong as prices are usually lower and in more remote areas people may be unaware of the exchange rate. Also, to ordinary Vietnamese, 18,000d is a lot of money, while US$1 means nothing.

ATMs are plentiful in HCMC and Hanoi and are now pretty ubiquitous in other major tourist centres, but it is a good idea to travel with US dollars cash as a back up.

Try to avoid tatty notes. ATM withdrawals are limited to 2 million dong per transaction. Banks in the main centres will change other major currencies including UK sterling, Hong Kong dollars, Thai baht, Swiss francs, Euros, Australian dollars, Singapore dollars and Canadian dollars. **Credit cards** are increasingly accepted, particularly Visa, MasterCard, Amex and JCB. Large hotels, expensive restaurants and medical centres invariably take them but beware a surcharge of between 2.5% and 4.5%. Most hotels will not add a surcharge onto your bill if paying by credit card. Traveller's cheques are best denominated in US dollars and can only be cashed in banks in the major towns. Commission of 2-4% is payable if cashing into dollars but not if you are converting them direct to dong.

Cost of travelling
On a budget expect to pay around US$6-15 per night for accommodation and about US$6-12 for food. A good mid-range hotel will cost US$12-30. There are comfort and cost levels anywhere from here up to more than US$200 per night. For travelling, many use the Open Tour Buses as they are inexpensive and, by Vietnamese standards, 'safe'. Slightly more expensive are trains followed by planes.

Opening hours
Banks Mon-Fri 0800-1600. Many close 1100-1300 or 1130-1330.
Offices Mon-Fri 0730-1130, 1330-1630.
Restaurants, **cafés**, **bars** Daily from 0700 or 0800 although some open earlier. Bars are supposed to close at 2400 by law.
Shops Daily 0800-2000. Some stay open for another hour, especially in tourist centres.

Police and the law
If you are robbed in Vietnam, report the incident to the police (for your insurance claim). Otherwise, the police are of no use whatsoever. They will do little or nothing (apart from log the crime on an incident sheet that you will need for your claim).

Vietnam is not the best place to come into conflict with the law. Avoid getting arrested. If you are arrested, however, ask for consular assistance and English-speaking staff.

Involvement in politics, possession of political material, business activities that have not been licensed by appropriate authorities, or non-sanctioned religious activities (including proselytizing) can result in detention. Sponsors of small, informal religious gatherings such as bible-study groups in hotel rooms, as well as distributors of religious materials, have been detained, fined and expelled (source: US State Department). The army are extremely sensitive about all their military buildings and become exceptionally irate if you take a photo. Indeed there are signs to this effect outside all military installations.

Post
Postal services are pretty good. Post offices open daily 0700-2100; smaller ones close for lunch. Outgoing packages are opened and checked by the censor.

Safety
Travel advisories
The US State Department's travel advisory: **Travel Warnings & Consular Information Sheets**, www.travel.state.gov, and the **UK Foreign and Commonwealth Office**'s travel warning section, www.fco.gov.uk, are useful. Do not take any valuables on to the streets of HCMC as bag and jewellery snatching is a common problem. Thieves work in teams, often with beggar women carrying babies as a decoy. Beware of people who obstruct your path (pushing a bicycle across the pavement is a common ruse); your pockets are being emptied from behind. Young men on fast motorbikes also cruise the central streets of HCMC waiting to pounce on victims. The situation in other cities is not so bad but take care in Nha Trang and Hanoi. Never go by cyclo in a strange part of town after dark.

Lone women travellers have fewer problems than in many other Asian countries. The most common form of harassment usually consists of comic and harmless displays of macho behaviour.

Unexploded ordnance is still a threat in some areas. It is best not to stray too far from the beaten track and don't unearth bits of suspicious metal.

Single Western men will be targeted by prostitutes on street corners, in tourist bars and those cruising on motorbikes.

Beware of the following scams: being overcharged on credit cards; the pretend tearing up of a credit card transaction and the issuing of a new one; massage parlours where your money is stolen when you're having a massage; newspapers being sold for 5 times their value; and motorbikes that go 'wrong' and need repairs costing the earth.

Telephone
Telephone numbers beginning with 091 or 090 are mobile phone numbers. Vietnam's IDD is 0084; directory enquiries: 1080; operator-assisted domestic long-distance calls 103; international directory enquiries 143; yellow pages 1081.

To make a domestic call dial 0 + area code + phone number. Note that all numbers in this guide include the area code. Most shops or cafés will let you call a local number for 2000d; look for the blue sign 'dien thoai cong cong' (public telephone). All post offices provide international telephone services. The cost of calls has been greatly reduced but some post offices and hotels still insist on charging for a minimum of 3 mins. You start paying for an overseas call from the moment you ring even if the call is not answered. By dialling 171 or 178 followed by 0 or 00 to make an international call, it is around 30% cheaper.

Pay-as-you-go sim cards are available from a number of operators including **Mobiphone** and **Vinaphone**. A sim card costs around £10 and top-up cards are available. Calls are very cheap and it's the most convenient and cheapest way to keep in touch in country.

Time

Vietnam is 7 hrs ahead of GMT.

Tipping

Vietnamese do not normally tip if eating in small restaurants but may tip in expensive bars. Foreigners leave small change, which is appreciated. Big hotels and restaurants add 5-10% service charge and the government tax of 10% to the bill. Taxis are rounded up to the nearest 5000d, hotel porters 20,000d.

Tourist information

Contact details for tourist offices and other resources are given in the relevant Ins and outs sections throughout the text.

The national tourist office is **Vietnam National Administration of Tourism** (www.vietnamtourism.com), whose role is to promote Vietnam as a tourist destination rather than to provide tourist information. Visitors to its offices can get some information and maps but they are more likely to be offered tours. Good tourist information is available from tour operators in the main tourist centres.

Visas and immigration

Tourist visa extensions need careful planning as, although hotels will accept photocopies of passports and visas, you cannot buy a ticket or fly with Vietnam Airlines without the original.

Valid passports with visas issued by a Vietnamese embassy are required by all visitors, irrespective of citizenship. Visas are normally valid only for arrival by air at Hanoi and HCMC. Those wishing to enter or leave Vietnam by land must specify the border crossing when applying. It is possible to alter the point of departure at immigration offices in Hanoi and HCMC. Contact the Vietnamese

embassy in your country for specific application details. Visas on arrival at land crossings are not available and visas on arrival at airports are not exactly as they appear; they must be arranged in advance with licensed companies, paperwork signed before arriving and handed at desks at airports to get the visa. This may or may not work out cheaper than the embassy approach.

The standard tourist visa is valid for 1 month for 1 entry (*mot lan*) only. Tourist visas cost £44 and generally take 5 days to process. Express visas cost more and take 2 days. 2-month tourist visas are now available for £85. If you are planning on staying for a while or making a side trip to Laos or Cambodia with the intention of coming back to Vietnam then a 1-month multiple entry visa will make life much simpler. Business visas cost the same as multiple entry visas. Visa regulations are ever changing; usually it is possible to extend visas within Vietnam. Travel agencies and hotels will probably add their own mark-up but for many people it is worth paying to avoid the difficulty of making 1 or 2 journeys to an embassy. Visas can be extended for 1 month. Depending on where you are it will take between 1 day and a week. A visa valid for 1 month can only be extended for 1 month; a further 1 month extension is then possible. Citizens of Sweden, Norway, Denmark, and Finland may visit, visa free, for not more than 15 days.

Vietnam now operate a quasi 'visa on arrival' programme. An online application must be made through a company such as www.visa-vietnam.org. A pre-approved letter is granted and a service fee paid but payment for the actual visa is made on collection at the airport.

Contents

Footprint features

Ho Chi Minh City

Ins and outs

Getting there

Ho Chi Minh City (HCMC) may not be Vietnam's capital, but it is the economic powerhouse of the country and the largest city. Reflecting its premier economic position, it is well connected with the wider world – indeed, more airlines fly into here than into Hanoi; it is also connected to all the domestic airports bar one. **Tan Son Nhat Airport** is 30-40 minutes from the centre. By taxi the cost is around US$6-7. Taxi drivers may try to demand a flat fee in US dollars but you should insist on using the meter, which is the law, and pay in dong. The official flat fare to downtown organized through a desk at the airport is US$8.

The **railway station** is northwest of the city centre and there are regular daily connections with Hanoi and all stops on the line north. As well as international air connections, there are bus services to Phnom Penh (Cambodia). Buses for destinations within the country leave from two main city **bus terminals** and connect Ho Chi Minh City with many larger towns in the central and northern regions, and with most places in the Mekong Delta. With the ring road around Ho Chi Minh City, few long-distance public buses actually come into town. To avoid an additional 45-minute journey, try to catch a bus heading to Ben Xe Mien Dong or join the large number of visitors who arrive in Ho Chi Minh City on one or other of the many competing **Open Tour Buses**. ▸▸ *See Transport, page 63.*

Getting around

Ho Chi Minh City has abundant transport – which is fortunate, because it is a hot, large and increasingly polluted city. Metered taxis, motorcycle taxis and a handful of cyclos vie for business in a healthy spirit of competition. Many tourists who prefer some level of independence opt to hire (or even, buy) a bicycle or motorbike. ▸▸ *See Tour operators, page 59.*

Orientation

Virtually all of Ho Chi Minh City lies to the west of the Saigon River. The eastern side of the river, District 2, is for the most part marshy, poor and rather squalid, although a growing expat city has evolved. Most visitors to the city head straight for hotels in Districts 1 (the historic centre) or 3. Many will arrive on buses in De Tham or Pham Ngu Lao streets, the backpacker area, in District 1, not far from the city centre. Cholon or Chinatown (District 5) is a mile west of the centre. The Port of Saigon lies downstream of the city centre in districts 4 and 8. Few visitors venture here although cruise ships berth in District 4.

Safety

It is not safe to carry handbags and purses on the streets of Ho Chi Minh City. Drive-by snatchings are on the increase. Jewellery should not be worn. Cameras should be held tightly at all times and passports, tickets and money kept in the safe of your hotel.

Tourist information

A **Tourist Information Center** ⓘ *92-96 Nguyen Hue St, T8-8322 6033, www.ticvietnam. com, daily 0800-2100*, provides free information, hotel reservations, an ATM and currency exchange and free internet.

History

Before the 15th century, Saigon was a small Khmer village surrounded by a wilderness of forest and swamp. Through the years it had ostensibly been incorporated into the Funan and then the Khmer empires, although it is hard to believe that these kingdoms had any direct, long-term influence on the inhabitants of the community. The Khmers, who called the region *Prei Nokor*, used the area for hunting.

By 1623 Saigon had become an important commercial centre, and in the mid-17th century it became the residence of the so-called Vice-King of Cambodia. In 1698, the Viets managed to extend their control this far south and finally Saigon was brought under Vietnamese control and hence celebrated the city's tercentenary in 1998. By 1790, the city had a population of 50,000 and before Hué was selected as the capital of the Nguyen Dynasty, Emperor Gia Long made Saigon his place of residence.

In the middle of the 19th century, the French began to challenge Vietnamese authority in the south of Vietnam and Saigon. Between 1859 and 1862, in response to the Nguyen persecution of Catholics in Vietnam, the French attacked and captured Saigon, along with the southern provinces of Vinh Long, An Giang and Ha Tien. The Treaty of Saigon in 1862 ratified the conquest and created the new French colony of Cochin China. Saigon was developed in French style: wide, tree-lined boulevards, street-side cafés, elegant French architecture, boutiques and the smell of baking baguettes. The map of French Saigon in the 1930s was a city that owed more to Haussmann than Vietnamese geomancers.

Today

The population of Ho Chi Minh City today is officially more than seven million and rising fast as the rural poor are lured by the tales of streets paved with gold. Actual numbers are thought to be considerably higher when all the recent migrants without residence cards are added. But it has been a roller-coaster ride over the last 40 years. During the course of the Vietnam War, as refugees spilled in from a devastated countryside, the population of Saigon almost doubled from 2.4 million in 1965 to around 4.5 million by 1975. With reunification in 1976, the new communist authorities pursued a policy of depopulation, believing that the city had become too large, that it was parasitic and was preying on the surrounding countryside. Certainly, most of the jobs were in the service sector, and were linked to the United States' presence. For example, Saigon had 56,000 registered prostitutes alone (and many, many, more unregistered), most of them country girls.

Vietnam's economic reforms are most in evidence in Ho Chi Minh City and the average annual income here, at US$2800, is more than double the national average (US$1000). It is here that the highest concentration of Hoa (ethnic Chinese) is to be found – numbering around 380,000 – and, although once persecuted for their economic success, they still have the greatest economic influence and acumen. Most of Ho Chi Minh City's ethnic Chinese live in the district of Cholon, and from there control two-thirds of small-scale commercial enterprises. The reforms have encouraged the Hoa to begin investing in business again. Drawing on their links with fellow Chinese in Taiwan, Hong Kong, Bangkok and among the overseas Vietnamese, they are viewed by the government as crucial in improving prospects for the economy. The reforms have also brought economic inefficiencies into the open. Although the changes have brought wealth to a few, and increased the range of goods on sale, they have also created a much clearer division between the haves and the have-nots.

In its short history Saigon has had a number of keepers. Each has rebuilt the city in their own style. First the Khmer, then the early Vietnamese, followed by the French who tore it all down and started from scratch and were succeeded by the Americans and the 'Puppet' Regime, and finally the communist north who engineered society rather than the buildings, locking the urban fabric in a time warp.

Under the current regime, best described as crony capitalist, the city is once more being rebuilt. Ever larger holes are being torn in the heart of central Ho Chi Minh City. Whereas a few years ago it was common to see buildings disappear, now whole blocks fall to the wrecker's ball. From the holes left behind, concrete, steel and glass monuments emerge. There is, of course, a difference from earlier periods of remodelling of the city. Then, it was conducted on a human scale and the largest buildings, though grand, were on a scale that was in keeping with the dimensions of the streets and ordinary shophouses.

1 Ho Chi Minh City

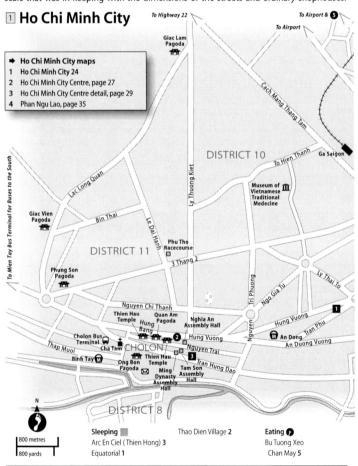

➡ Ho Chi Minh City maps
1 Ho Chi Minh City 24
2 Ho Chi Minh City Centre, page 27
3 Ho Chi Minh City Centre detail, page 29
4 Phan Ngu Lao, page 35

Sleeping ■
Arc En Ciel (Thien Hong) 3
Equatorial 1

Thao Dien Village 2

Eating ◆
Bu Tuong Xeo
Chan May 5

French buildings in Dong Khoi Street, for example, were consistent with the Vietnamese way of life: street-level trading with a few residential floors above. Now glitzy modern buildings on an altogether vaster scale dwarf every building from an earlier age. The latest overblown development is Times Square opposite the Grand Hotel on Dong Khoi St.

Ho Chi Minh City is divided, administratively, into 12 urban districts, or *quan*, and nine suburban districts, or *huyen*. These are further sub-divided into wards and the wards into neighbourhoods; each district and ward has its own People's Committee or local government who guard and protect their responsibilities and rights jealously and maintain a high degree of administrative autonomy. A city-wide People's Committee, elected every four years, oversees the functioning of the entire metropolis.

The future growth of Ho Chi Minh City will focus mostly on the southern and eastern sides. Saigon port did extend right up into the heart of the city into District 4 but has been

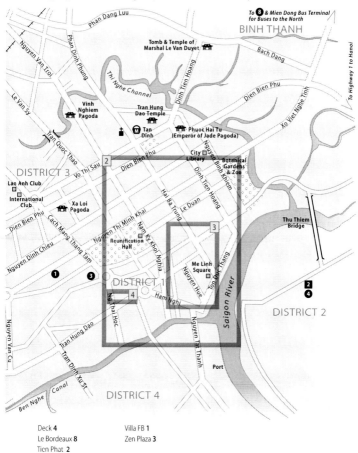

Deck **4**
Le Bordeaux **8**
Tien Phat **2**

Villa FB **1**
Zen Plaza **3**

relocated to Cat Lai and Hiep Phuoc in the suburbs. It is almost certain that in the coming years the valuable riverfront sites will be developed into desirable flats and offices – rather like London's Docklands. To the south, Saigon South, a huge new flank of the city is rising out of the marsh and mangrove. A site of 1336 ha has so far been converted from swamp into 'executive homes' and international schools; the infrastructure that will support the livelihoods of hundreds of thousands of people is materializing out of nothing. It may sound like propaganda but the fact is that parcels of what was recently disregarded wasteland are now changing hands for millions of dollars. Serious investors and land speculators are moving in and the city is expanding fast. Land prices in District 2, the marshy area to the east of the Saigon River, soared to previously unimaginable heights as speculators snapped up land in advance of the construction of new river crossings.

Sights

All the sights of Central Ho Chi Minh City can be reached on foot in no more than 30 minutes from the major hotel areas of Nguyen Hue, Dong Khoi and Ton Duc Thang streets. Visiting all the sights described below will take several days, not that we would particularly recommend visiting them all. Quite a good first port of call, however, is the **Panorama 33 Café** on the 33rd floor of **Saigon Trade Center** ① *37 Ton Duc Thang St, Mon-Fri 1100-2400, Sat-Sun 0900-2400*. From this vantage point you can see the whole city stretching before you, and its position and layout in relation to the river and surrounding swampland becomes strikingly clear. Another good spot to survey the river and downtown building work, is Chique, 15th floor, Landmark Building, 5B Ton Duc Thang St, 1400-2300. Its interior isn't chic but the views are front row. ▸▸ *For listings, see page 45-66.*

City centre

The core of Ho Chi Minh City is, in many respects, the most interesting and historical. Remember, of course, that 'historical' here has a very different meaning from that in Hanoi. In Ho Chi Minh City a 100-year-old building is ancient – and, alas, increasingly rare. Still, a saunter down **Dong Khoi Street**, in District 1, the old rue Catinat can still give one an impression of life in a more elegant and less frenzied era. Much remains on a small and personal scale and within a 100-m radius of just about anywhere on Dong Khoi or Thai Van Lung streets there are dozens of cafés, restaurants and increasingly snazzy boutiques. However, the character of the street has altered with the opening of luxury chain names and will alter further with the completion of the Times Square mega hotel development. A little bit of Graham Greene history was lost in 2010 when the Givral Café in the Eden Centre, which featured in *A Quiet American*, was closed as Vincom Towers built another tower block on Lam Son Square.

Lam Son Square and around
The once-impressive, French-era **Opera House** (**Nha Hat Thanh Pho**) ① *7 Lam Son Sq, T8-3832 2009, nhahat_ghvk@hcm.fpt.vn*, dominates Lam Son Square. It was built in 1897 to the design of French architect Ferret Eugene and restored in 1998. It once housed the National Assembly; nowadays, when it is open, it provides a varied programme of events, for example, traditional theatre, contemporary dance and gymnastics.

North of the Opera House is the repainted **Continental Hotel**, built in 1880 and an

② Ho Chi Minh City centre

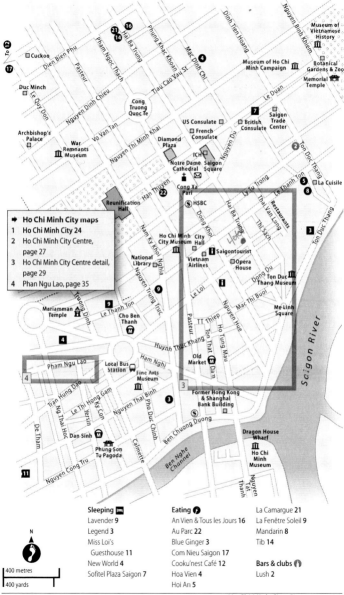

Ho Chi Minh City maps

1 Ho Chi Minh City 24
2 Ho Chi Minh City Centre, page 27
3 Ho Chi Minh City Centre detail, page 29
4 Phan Ngu Lao, page 35

Sleeping 🛏
Lavender 9
Legend 3
Miss Loi's
  Guesthouse 11
New World 4
Sofitel Plaza Saigon 7

Eating 🍴
An Vien & Tous les Jours 16
Au Parc 22
Blue Ginger 3
Com Nieu Saigon 17
Cooku'nest Café 12
Hoa Vien 4
Hoi An 5

La Camargue 21
La Fenêtre Soleil 9
Mandarin 8
Tib 14

Bars & clubs 🍸
Lush 2

integral part of the city's history. Graham Greene stayed here and the hotel features in the novel *The Quiet American*. Old journalists' haunt **Continental Shelf** was "a famous verandah where correspondents, spies, speculators, traffickers, intellectuals and soldiers used to meet during the war to glean information and pick up secret reports, half false, half true or half disclosed. All of this is more than enough for it to be known as Radio Catinat". It has a delightful enclosed garden ("I sometimes went there for a late evening drink among the frangipani and hibiscus blossom ... It was the reverse of the frenzy of the war, and a good place to think," wrote war journalist Jon Swain).

The **Continental** lines **Dong Khoi Street** (formerly the bar-lined Tu Do Street, the old Rue Catinat), which stretches from Cong Xa Paris down to the river. All the shops specialize in, or sell a mix of silk clothes and accessories, jewellery, lacquerware and household goods. Facing the **Continental**, also adjoining Dong Khoi Street, is the opulent **Hotel Caravelle**, which houses boutique shops selling luxury goods. The **Caravelle** opened for business in 1959. The famous **Saigon Saigon** bar on the 10th floor was a favourite spot for wartime reporters and during the 1960s the *Associated Press*, *NBC*, *CBS*, the *New York Times* and *Washington Post* based their offices here. The press escaped casualties when, on 25 August 1964, a bomb exploded in room 514, on a floor mostly used by foreign reporters. The hotel suffered damage and there were injuries but the journalists were all out in the field. It was renamed **Doc Lap** (Independence Hotel) in 1975 but not before a Vietnamese tank trundled down the rue Catinat to Place Garnier (now Lam Son Square) and aimed its turret at the hotel; to this day nobody knows why it did not fire. During the filming of Graham Greene's *The Quiet American*, actors Michael Caine and Brendan Fraser stayed at the hotel.

At the northwest end of Nguyen Hue Boulevard is the yellow and white **City Hall**, formerly the French **Hôtel de Ville** built in 1897 and now the Ho Chi Minh City People's Committee building, which overlooks a **statue of Bac Ho** (Uncle Ho) offering comfort, or perhaps advice, to a child. This is a favourite spot for Vietnamese to have their photograph taken, especially newly-weds who believe old Ho confers some sort of blessing.

South of City Hall, the **Rex Hotel**, a pre-Liberation favourite with US officers, stands at the intersection of Le Loi and Nguyen Hue boulevards. This was the scene of the daily 'Five O'Clock Follies' where the military briefed an increasingly sceptical press corps during the Vietnam War. Fully renovated and smartly expanding, the crown on the fifth-floor terrace of the **Rex** (a good place to have a beer) is rotating once again following a number of years of immobility. Some maintain that it symbolizes Ho Chi Minh City's newly discovered (or rediscovered) vitality.

On weekend evenings thousands of young Saigon men and women and young families cruise up and down Nguyen Hue and Le Loi boulevards and Dong Khoi Street on motorbikes; this whirl of people and machines is known as *chay long rong* 'cruising' or *song voi*, 'living fast'. There are now so many motorbikes on the streets of Ho Chi Minh City that intersections seem lethally confused. Miraculously, the riders miss each other (most of the time) while pedestrians safely make their way through waves of machines.

Notre Dame Cathedral

ⓘ *Visiting times are described as being 0500-1100 and 1500-1730. Communion is celebrated here 7 times on Sun (drawing congregations Western churches can only dream of) and 3 times on weekdays.*

North up Dong Khoi Street, in the middle of **Cong Xa Paris** (Paris Square), is the imposing, austere red-brick, twin-spired Notre Dame Cathedral, overlooking a grassed square in which a statue of the Virgin Mary stands holding an orb. The statue was the subject

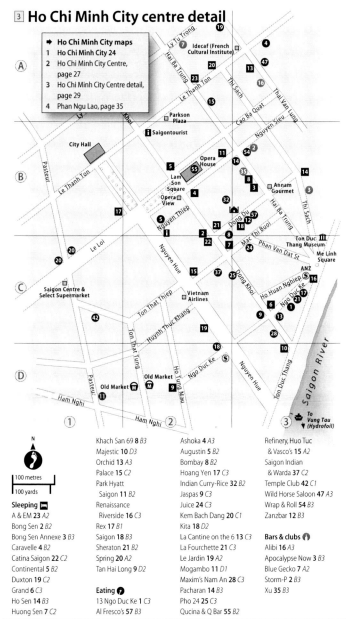

➡ **Ho Chi Minh City maps**
1 Ho Chi Minh City 24
2 Ho Chi Minh City Centre,
    page 27
3 Ho Chi Minh City Centre detail,
    page 29
4 Phan Ngu Lao, page 35

N
100 metres
100 yards

Sleeping 🛏
A & EM **23** *A2*
Bong Sen **2** *B2*
Bong Sen Annexe **3** *B3*
Caravelle **4** *B2*
Catina Saigon **22** *C2*
Continental **5** *B2*
Duxton **19** *C2*
Grand **6** *C3*
Ho Sen **14** *B3*
Huong Sen **7** *C2*
Khach San 69 **8** *B3*
Majestic **10** *D3*
Orchid **13** *A3*
Palace **15** *C2*
Park Hyatt
   Saigon **11** *B2*
Renaissance
   Riverside **16** *C3*
Rex **17** *B1*
Saigon **18** *B3*
Sheraton **21** *B2*
Spring **20** *A2*
Tan Hai Long **9** *D2*

Eating 🍴
13 Ngo Duc Ke **1** *C3*
Al Fresco's **57** *B3*
Ashoka **4** *A3*
Augustin **5** *B2*
Bombay **8** *B2*
Hoang Yen **17** *C3*
Indian Curry-Rice **32** *B2*
Jaspas **9** *C3*
Juice **24** *C3*
Kem Bach Dang **20** *C1*
Kita **18** *D2*
La Cantine on the 6 **13** *C3*
La Fourchette **21** *C3*
Le Jardin **19** *A2*
Mogambo **11** *D1*
Maxim's Nam An **28** *C3*
Pacharan **14** *B3*
Pho 24 **25** *C3*
Qucina & Q Bar **55** *B2*
Refinery, Huo Tuc
   & Vasco's **15** *A2*
Saigon Indian
   & Warda **37** *C2*
Temple Club **42** *C1*
Wild Horse Saloon **47** *A3*
Wrap & Roll **54** *B3*
Zanzbar **12** *B3*

Bars & clubs 🍸
Alibi **16** *A3*
Apocalypse Now **3** *B3*
Blue Gecko **7** *A2*
Storm-P **2** *B3*
Xu **35** *B3*

of intense scrutiny in 2006 as it was said that it had shed tears. The cathedral was built between 1877 and 1880 and is said to be on the site of an ancient pagoda. A number of the homeless sleep within its walls at night; unfortunately the signs asking Vietnamese men not to treat the walls as a public urinal do not deter this unpleasant but widespread practice. Mass times are a spectacle as crowds, unable to squeeze through the doors, listen to the service while perched on their parked motorbikes in rows eight or nine deep.

General Post Office

ⓘ *2 Cong Xa Paris, daily 0730-1930.*

Facing onto the Paris Square is the General Post Office, built in the 1880s in French style, it is a particularly distinguished building. The front façade has attractive cornices with French and Khmer motifs and the names of notable French men of letters and science. Inside, the high, vaulted ceiling and fans create a deliciously cool atmosphere in which to scribble a postcard. Note the old wall-map of Cochin China that has miraculously survived. The enormous portrait of Ho Chi Minh, hanging at the end of the hall, completes the sense of grandeur.

Reunification Hall

ⓘ *135 Nam Ky Khoi Nghia St, T8-3822 3652, daily 0730-1100, 1300-1600, 15,000d, brochure 10000d, documentary 50,000d. The guides are friendly, but their English is not always very good. Tours every 10 mins. The hall is sometimes closed for state occasions.*

Ngo Dinh Diem's **Presidential Palace**, now renamed Reunification Hall, or the **Thong Nhat Conference Hall**, is in a large park to the southeast of Nguyen Thi Minh Khai Street and southwest of Nam Ky Khoi Nghia Street. The residence of the French governor was built on this site in 1868 and was later renamed the Presidential Palace. In February 1962, a pair of planes took off to attack Viet Cong emplacements – piloted by two of the south's finest airmen – but they turned back to bomb the Presidential Palace in a futile attempt to assassinate President Diem. The president, who held office between 1955-1963, escaped with his family to the cellar, but the palace had to be demolished and replaced with a new building. (Diem was later assassinated after a military coup.) One of the two pilots, Nguyen Thanh Trung is a Vice President of **Vietnam Airlines** and still flies government officials around every couple of months to keep his pilot's licence current. One of the most memorable photographs taken during the war was of a North Vietnamese Army (NVA) tank crashing through the gates of the Palace on 30 April 1975 – symbolizing the end of South Vietnam and its government. The President of South Vietnam, General Duong Van Minh, along with his entire cabinet, was arrested in the Palace shortly afterwards. The hall has been preserved as it was found in 1975 and visitors can take a guided tour. In the **Vice President's Guest Room**, there is a lacquered painting of the Temple of Literature in Hanoi, while the **Presenting of Credentials Room** contains a fine 40-piece lacquer work showing diplomats presenting their credentials during the Le Dynasty (15th century). In the basement there are operations rooms, military maps, radios and other paraphernalia. In essence, it is a 1960s-style building filled with 1960s-style official furnishings that now look very kitsch. Not only was the building designed according to the principles of Chinese geomancy but the colour of the carpets – lurid mustard yellow in one room – was also chosen depending on whether it was to calm or stimulate users of the rooms. Visitors are shown an interesting film about the Revolution and some fascinating photographs and memorabilia from the era. A replica of the tank that bulldozed through the gates of the compound heralding the end of South Vietnam is displayed in the forecourt.

War Remnants Museum

ⓘ *28 Vo Van Tan St, Q3, T8-3930 6325, daily 0730-1200, 1330-1700, 15,000d.*

All the horrors of the Vietnam War from the nation's perspective – photographs of atrocities and action, bombs, military tanks and planes and deformed foetuses – are piled up in a new museum building. In the courtyard are tanks, bombs and helicopters, while the new museum, arranged in five new sections, records man's inhumanity. The display covers the Son My (My Lai) massacre on 16 March 1968, the effects of napalm and phosphorous, and the after-effects of Agent Orange defoliation (this is particularly disturbing, with bottled malformed human foetuses). There's also a new feature on Senator John Kerry's Vietnam involvement. Unsurprisingly, there is no record of North Vietnamese atrocities to US and South Vietnamese troops. This museum has gone through some interesting name changes in recent years. It began life as the Exhibition House of American and Chinese War Crimes. In 1990, 'Chinese' was dropped from the name, and in 1994 'American' was too. Since 1996 it has simply been called the War Remnants Museum.

Archbishop's Palace

ⓘ *330 Nguyen Dinh Chieu St and corner of Tran Quoc Thao St.*

Around this area are a number of very fine French-era buildings still standing; some have been allowed to fall into decay but others have been well maintained. In particular the Archbishop's Palace and the high schools, **Le Qui Don** ⓘ *2 Le Qui Don St*, and **Marie Curie** ⓘ *Nam Ky Khoi Nghia St*. All have had extensions built in recent years, but at least the schools (unlike the archbishop) have attempted to blend the new buildings in with the old. The palace is believed to be the oldest house in Ho Chi Minh City, built in 1790 (although not originally on this spot) for the then French bishop of Adran, Pierre Pigneau de Behaine.

Xa Loi Pagoda

ⓘ *89 Ba Huyen Thanh Quan St, daily 0630-1100, 1430-1700.*

Ho Chi Minh City has close to 200 pagodas – far too many for most visitors to see. Many of the finest are in Cholon (see page 35), although there is a selection closer to the main hotel area in central Ho Chi Minh City. The Xa Loi Pagoda is not far from the War Remnants Museum and is surrounded by food stalls. Built in 1956, the pagoda contains a multi-storeyed tower, which is particularly revered, as it houses a relic of the Buddha. The main sanctuary contains a large, bronze-gilded Buddha in an attitude of meditation. Around the walls are a series of silk paintings depicting the previous lives of the Buddha (with an explanation of each life to the right of the entrance into the sanctuary). The pagoda is historically, rather than artistically, important as it became a focus of dissent against the Diem regime (see box, page 37).

Le Duan Street

North of the cathedral is Le Duan Street, the former corridor of power with Ngo Dinh Diem's Palace at one end, the zoo at the other and the former embassies of the three major powers, France, the USA and the UK, in between. Quite who was aping who and who was the puppet and who was the master was a tangled question. Nearest the Reunification Hall is the compound of the **French Consulate**. A block away is the **former US Embassy**. After diplomatic ties were resumed in 1995 the Americans lost little time in demolishing the 1960s building which held so many bad memories. The US Consulate General now stands on this site. Outside, a queue of hopeful visa supplicants forms every day come rain or shine. This office has the distinction of being the busiest overseas US mission for marriage visas, a title for which it vies closely with the US Embassy in Manila. A **memorial** outside, on the corner of Mac Dinh Chi Street, records the attack by Viet Cong special forces during the Tet offensive of 1968 and the final victory in 1975. On the other side of the road, a little further northeast at 25 Le Duan, is the **former British Embassy**, erected in the late 1950s, now the British Consulate General and British Council. At 2 Le Duan Street is the **Museum of Ho Chi Minh Campaign** (Bao Tang Quan Doi) ① *T8-3822 9387, Tue-Sun 0730-1100, 1330-1630, 15,000d,* with a tank and warplane in the front compound. It contains an indifferent display of photographs and articles of war.

Botanical Gardens and Zoo

① *2 Nguyen Binh Khiem St, T8-3829 3728, daily 0700-2000, entrance to gardens and zoo, 12,000d.*

At the end of Le Duan Street are the Botanical Gardens which run alongside Nguyen Binh Khiem Street at the point where the Thi Nghe channel flows into the Saigon River. The gardens were established in 1864 by French botanist Jean-Batiste Louis Pierre; by the 1970s they had a collection of nearly 2000 species, and a particularly fine display of orchids. With the dislocations of the immediate postwar years, the gardens went into decline, a situation from which they are still trying to recover. In the south quarter of the gardens is a mediocre zoo with a rather moth-eaten collection of animals which form a backdrop to smartly dressed Vietnamese families posing for photographs.

Museum of Vietnamese History

① *2 Nguyen Binh Khiem St, T8-3829 8146, www.baotanglichsuvn.com, Tue-Sun 0800-1130, 1330-1700,15,000d. Photography permit, 32,000d. Labels in English and French. Water puppet shows (see also page 56) are held here daily 0900, 1000, 1100, 1400, 1500 and 1600, 15 mins, US$2.*

The history museum (Bao Tang Lich Su Viet Nam) is an elegant building constructed in 1928 and is pagodaesque in style. It displays a wide range of artefacts from the prehistoric (300,000 years ago) and the Dongson periods (3500 BC-AD 100), right through to the birth of the Vietnamese Communist Party in 1930. Particularly impressive are the Cham sculptures, of which the standing bronze Buddha, dating from the fourth to sixth century, is probably the finest. There is also a delicately carved Devi (Goddess) dating from the 10th century as well as pieces such as the head of Shiva, Hindu destroyer and creator, from the eighth to ninth century and Ganesh, elephant-headed son of Shiva and Parvati, also dating from the eighth to ninth century.

There are also representative pieces from the Chen-la, Funan, Khmer, Oc-eo and Han Chinese periods, and from the various Vietnamese dynasties together with some hill tribe artefacts. Labelling is in English, French and Vietnamese.

Other highlights include the wooden stakes planted in the Bach Dang riverbed for repelling the war ships of the Mongol Yuan in the 13th century, a beautiful Phoenix head from the Tran dynasty (13th to 14th century) and an Hgor (big drum) from the Jarai people, made from the skin of two elephants. It belonged to the Potauoui (King of Fire) family in Ajunpa district, Gia Lai Province. There are some fine sandstone sculptures too including an incredibly smooth linga from Long An Province (seventh to eighth century) in the Mekong Delta. The linga represents the cult of Siva and signifies gender, energy, fertility and potency.

Near the History Museum is the **Memorial Temple** ① *Tue-Sun 0800-1130, 1300-1600,* constructed in 1928 and dedicated to famous Vietnamese.

Ho Chi Minh City Museum and around

ⓘ 65 Ly Tu Trong St, T8-3829 9741, www.hcmc-museum.edu.vn, daily 0800-1700

This museum includes a mixed bag of displays concerning the revolution, with a display of photographs, a few pieces of hardware (helicopter, anti-aircraft guns) in the back compound, and some memorabilia. Other exhibits chart the development of the city and its economy. The building itself is historically important. Dominating a prominent intersection, the grey-white classical French-designed building was built as a museum before it became the palace for the governor of Cochin China in 1890. After the 1945 revolution it was used for administrative offices before returning to the French as the High Commissioner's residence in September 1945. During the War, Ngo Dinh Diem resided here under its new name as Southern Governor's Palace; during the reign of Nguyen Van Thieu (1967-1975), it operated as the supreme court.

Southwest from the museum on the corner of Ly Tu Trong Street and Nam Ky Khoi Nghia is the National Library.

Mariamman Hindu Temple

ⓘ 45 Truong Dinh St.

Although clearly Hindu, with a statue of Mariamman flanked by Maduraiveeran and Pechiamman, the temple is largely frequented by Chinese worshippers, providing the strange sight of Chinese Vietnamese clasping incense sticks and prostrating themselves in front of a Hindu deity, as they would to a Buddha image. The Chinese have always been pragmatic when it comes to religions.

Ben Thanh Market (Cho Ben Thanh)

A large, covered central market, Ben Thanh Market faces a statue of Tran Nguyen Han (a Le Dynasty general) at a large and chaotic roundabout, the Ben Thanh gyratory system, which marks the intersection of Le Loi, Ham Nghi and Tran Hung Dao streets. Ben Thanh is well stocked with clothes (cheap souvenir T-shirts), household goods, a wide range of soap, shampoo and sun cream, a good choice of souvenirs, lacquerware, embroidery and so on, as well as some terrific lines in food, including cold meats, fresh and dried fruits. It is not cheap (most local people window-shop here and purchase elsewhere) but the quality is high and the selection probably without equal. It is a terrific experience just to wander through and marvel at the range of produce on offer, all the more so now most of the beggars have been eased out. Outside the north gate (cua Bac) on Le Thanh Ton Street are some tempting displays of fruit (the oranges and apples are imported) and cut flowers.

The **Ben Thanh Night Market** has flourished since 2003. Starting at dusk and open until after midnight the night market is Ho Chi Minh City's attempt to recreate Bangkok's Patpong market. As the sun sinks and the main market closes stalls spring up in the surrounding streets. Clothes and cheap jewellery and an abundance of food stalls are the key attractions. The clear fact is that every night and often way beyond midnight the night market remains well and truly open. This may not sound unusual to new visitors but as the city authorities have been engaged in a tireless war against open-air eating for the past half dozen years the fact that it is now possible to sit in the open and eat well and cheaply is a positive achievement.

Opposite the south gate of Ben Thanh Market is a swirling current of traffic negotiating (by and large successfully) the Benh Thanh gyratory system, one of Ho Chi Minh City's busiest roundabouts and immediately to the south of that is the central (local) bus station. You can obtain a highly useful map inside the station and attempt to ask questions but y little English is spoken. Buses are air-conditioned too.

Ho Chi Minh City has a number of markets, but this one and the Binh Tay Market in Cholon (see page 39) are the largest. Many of the markets are surprisingly well stocked for a country that not too long ago was close to economic collapse.

Fine Arts Museum

ⓘ *97A Pho Duc Chinh St, T8-3829 4441, daily 0900-1700, 10,000d. Not everything is labelled and what is labelled is not in English*

The so-called Fine Arts Museum (Bao Tang My Thuat), housed in an impressive cream-coloured mansion is a distinctly unimpressive and unloved collection of dusty works of art. The third floor contains artefacts from the ancient civilizations of Oc-eo through to the Cham era. More recent collections include some attractive Dong Nai ceramics of the early 20th century. Highlights include a 12th-century sculpture of kala, a monster guarding the temple, from My Son. It is a fanged beast with a big protuberance for a nose, bulging eyes and forest-thick eyebrows. Hindu god sculptures are made of soft sandstone: Laksmi, found in Soc Trang in the Mekong Delta (seventh to eighth century) is the goddess of beauty and good fortune. A line of funeral statues (gaunt-looking, wooden folk) made by the Tay Nguyen people in the early 20th century in the central Highlands, line a corridor. These figures are crafted by the living as substitutes of their late relatives.

Part of the second floor is devoted to more recent events. Lacquered pictures appear, such as the interior of Cu Chi by Quach Phong (1997). There's a small collection of propaganda art posters (undated) and a vast bronze mural of the nation indicating anti-American sentiment by Nguyen Sang (undated). Some of the most interesting work is by Americans who have produced work that reflects on the war – namely montage and photographs. The ground floor is given over to temporary exhibitions.

The building itself is worthy of note having been built in the early 20th century by a Chinese man whose fortune was made by selling empty bottles.

Phung Son Tu Pagoda

ⓘ *338 Nguyen Cong Tru St.*

This is a small temple built just after the Second World War by Fukien Chinese; its most notable features are the wonderful painted entrance doors with their fearsome armed warriors. Incense spirals hang in the open well of the pagoda, which is dedicated to Ong Bon, the Guardian of Happiness and Virtue.

The **War Surplus Market (Dan Sinh)** ⓘ *Yersin between Nguyen Thai Binh St and Nguyen Cong Tru St*, is not far from the Phung Son Tu Pagoda. Merchandise on sale includes dog tags and military clothing and equipment (not all of it authentic). The market is popular with Western visitors looking for mementoes of their visit, so bargain particularly hard.

Old Market and riverside

The Old Market is on Ton That Dam Street, running between Ham Nghi Street and Ton That Thiep Street. It is the centre for the sale of black market goods (particularly consumer electronics) – now openly displayed. There is also a good range of foodstalls and fruit sellers. Close by is the old and rather splendid **Hong Kong and Shanghai Bank building** ⓘ *Ben Chuong Duong St*. It no longer houses the HSBC bank, which returned to Vietnam in 1994; this is now to be found on Dong Khoi Street facing the cathedral. Nguyen Tat Thanh Street runs south from here over the Ben Nghe Channel to **Dragon House Wharf**, at the confluence of the Ben Nghe Channel and the Saigon River. The former customs building, dating from 1863, has been converted into the **Ho Chi Minh Museum** ① *1 Nguyen Tat Thanh St, 0730-1130, 1330-1630, 10,000d,* (predominantly on the first floor), celebrating the life and exploits of Ho Chi Minh, mostly through pictures and the odd piece of memorabilia. School children are brought here to learn about their country's recent history, and people of all ages have their photographs taken with a portrait of Bac Ho in the background.

A short distance north up Ton Duc Thang Street from the broad Me Linh Square (in the centre of which is an imposing statue of Vietnamese hero Tran Hung Dao) is the rarely visited **Ton Duc Thang Museum** ① *5 Ton Duc Thang St, T8-3829 7542, Tue-Sun 0730-1130, 1330-1700, free.* Opened in 1989, it is dedicated to the life of Ton Duc Thang or Bac (Uncle) Ton. Bac Ton, a comrade who fought with Ho Chi Minh, was appointed President of Vietnam following Ho's death, remaining in office until his own death in 1980. The museum contains an array of photographs and other memorabilia.

Pham Ngu Lao

Most backpackers arriving overland in Ho Chi Minh City are dropped off in this bustling district, a 10- to 15-minute walk from downtown. Those arriving by air tend to head straight here too. The countless hotels, guesthouses and rooms to rent open and close and change name or owner with remarkable speed. The area is littered with restaurants, cafés, bars, email services, laundries, tour agencies and money changers, all fiercely competitive; there are mini-supermarkets and shops selling rucksacks, footwear, CDs, DVDs, pirated software and ethnic knick-knacks.

Cholon (Chinatown)

This is the heart of Ho Chi Minh City's Chinese community. Cholon is an area of commerce and trade; not global but nevertheless international. In

➡ **Ho Chi Minh City maps**
1 Ho Chi Minh City map 24
2 Ho Chi Minh City Centre, page 27
3 Ho Chi Minh City Centre detail, page 29
4 Pham Ngu Lao, page 35

4 **Pham Ngu Lao**

Not to scale

Sleeping 🛏
Hong Hoa **3**
Beautiful Saigon **4**
Linh **7**

Linh Thu Guesthouse **8**
Lucy **2**
Madame Cuc **20**
Mimi Guesthouse **10**
Minh Chau **11**
Que Huong
 (Liberty 3) **13**
Que Huong
 (Liberty 4) **14**

Eating 🍴
Café Zoom **9**
Cappuccino **2**
Good Morning
 Vietnam **13**
Kim Café **4**
Lac Thien **10**
Lucky **7**
Margharita **3**

Sozo **1**

Bars & clubs 🍸
Buffalo **8**
Cyclo **14**
Go2 **17**
Le Pub **15**
T&R Tavern **5**

typical Chinese style it is dominated by small and medium-size businesses and this shows in the buildings' shop fronts (look for the Chinese characters on signs over the door). The Chinese do less on the pavements than the Vietnamese and this is apparent on a tour through Cholon. Cholon is home to a great many temples and pagodas – some of which are described below. As one would expect from a Chinese trading district, there is plenty of fabric for sale in the markets.

Cho lon or 'big market' or Chinatown, is inhabited predominantly by Vietnamese of Chinese origin. However, since 1975 the authorities have alienated many Chinese, causing hundreds of thousands to leave the country. In making their escape many have died – either through drowning, as their perilously small and overladen craft foundered, or at the hands of pirates in the East Sea. In total, between 1977 and 1982, 709,570 refugees were recorded by the UNHCR as having fled Vietnam. By the late 1980s, the flow of boat people was being driven more by economic, rather than political, forces; there was little chance of making good in a country as poor, and in an economy as moribund, as that of Vietnam. Even with this flow of Chinese out of the country, there is still a large population of Chinese Vietnamese living in Cholon, an area which encompasses District 5 to the southwest of the city centre. Cholon appears to the casual visitor to be the most populated, noisiest and in general the most vigorous part of Ho Chi Minh City, if not of Vietnam. It is here that entrepreneurial talent and private funds are concentrated; both resources that the government are keen to mobilize in their attempts to reinvigorate the economy.

Cholon is worth visiting not only for the bustle and activity, but also because the temples and assembly halls found here are the finest in Ho Chi Minh City. As with any town in Southeast Asia boasting a sizeable Chinese population, the early settlers established meeting rooms which offered social, cultural and spiritual support to members of a dialect group. These assembly halls (*hoi quan*) are most common in Hoi An and Cholon. There are temples in the buildings which attract Vietnamese as well as Chinese worshippers, and indeed today serve little of their former purpose. The elderly meet here occasionally for a natter and a cup of tea.

Nghia An Assembly Hall
ⓘ *678 Nguyen Trai St, not far from the Arc en Ciel Hotel.*
A magnificent, carved, gold-painted wooden boat hangs over the entrance to the Nghia An Assembly Hall. To the left, on entering the temple, is a larger-than-life representation of Quan Cong's horse and groom. (Quan Cong was a loyal military man who lived in China in the third century.) At the main altar are three figures in glass cases: the central red-faced figure with a green cloak is Quan Cong himself; to the left and right are his trusty companions, General Chau Xuong (very fierce) and the mandarin Quan Binh respectively. On leaving, note the fine gold figures of guardians on the inside of the door panels.

Tam Son Assembly Hall
ⓘ *118 Trieu Quang Phuc St, just off Nguyen Trai St.*
The temple, built in the 19th century by Fukien immigrants, is frequented by childless women as it is dedicated to Chua Thai Sanh, the Goddess of Fertility. It is an uncluttered, 'pure' example of a Chinese/Vietnamese pagoda – peaceful and quiet. Like Nghia An Hoi Quan, the temple contains figures of Quan Cong, his horse and two companions.

Buddhist martyrs: self-immolation as protest

In August 1963 there was a demonstration of 15,000 people at the Xa Loi Pagoda, with speakers denouncing the Diem regime and telling jokes about Diem's sister-in-law, Madame Nhu (who was later to call monks "hooligans in robes"). Two nights later, ARVN special forces (from Roman Catholic families) raided the pagoda, battering down the gate, wounding 30 and killing seven people. Soon afterwards Diem declared martial law. The pagoda became a focus of discontent, with several monks committing suicide through self-immolation to protest against the Diem regime.

The first monk to immolate himself was 66-year-old Thich Quang Du, from Hué. On 11 June 1963, his companions poured petrol over him and set him alight as he sat in the lotus position. Pedestrians prostrated themselves at the sight; even a policeman threw himself to the ground in reverence. The next day, the picture of the monk in flames filled the front pages of newspapers around the world. Some 30 monks and nuns followed Thich's example in protesting against the Diem government and US involvement in South Vietnam. Two young US protesters also followed suit, one committing suicide by self-immolation outside the Pentagon and the other next to the UN, both in November 1968.

Madame Nhu, a Catholic, is reported as having said after the monks' death: "Let them burn, and we shall clap our hands." Within five months Diem had been killed in a military coup.

In May 1993, a Vietnamese man immolated himself at the Thien Mu Pagoda in Hué – the pagoda where the first monk-martyr was based.

Thien Hau Temples
ⓘ 710 and 802 Nguyen Trai St.

The Thien Hau Temple at 710 Nguyen Trai Street is one of the largest in the city. Constructed in the early 19th century, it is Chinese in inspiration and is dedicated to the worship of both the Buddha and to the Goddess Thien Hau, the goddess of the sea and the protector of sailors. Thien Hau was born in China and as a girl saved her father from drowning, but not her brother. Thien Hau's festival is marked here on the 23rd day of the third lunar month. One enormous incense urn and an incinerator can be seen through the main doors. Inside, the principal altar supports the gilded form of Thien Hau, with a boat to one side. Silk paintings depicting religious scenes decorate the walls. By far the most interesting part of the pagoda is the roof, which can be best seen from the small open courtyard. It must be one of the finest and most richly ornamented in Vietnam, with the high-relief frieze depicting episodes from the Legends of the Three Kingdoms. In the post-1975 era, many would-be refugees prayed here for safe deliverance before casting themselves adrift on the East Sea. A number of those who survived the perilous voyage sent offerings to the merciful goddess and the temple has been well maintained since. On busy days it is very smoky. Look up on leaving to see over the front door a picture of a boiling sea peppered with sinking boats. A benign Thien An looks down mercifully from a cloud. The temple has its own shop stocked with joss sticks, paper offerings and temple tat. Most people seem to buy their gear from the vendors outside who presumably don't have to pass on any 'overhead' costs. The shop also sells chilled water and Coca Cola.

A **second temple** dedicated to Thien Hau is a couple of blocks away at 802 Nguyen Trai St. This was built by migrants from Fukien Province in China in the 1730s although the

Betel nut

Betel nut has been a stimulant for the Vietnamese for hundreds of years. The ingredients combine the egg-shaped betel palm (*Areca catechu*) nut (*cau*) with Piper betel vine leaves (*trau*) and lime. When chewed (known as *An trau*) the ingredients stain the mouth and lips and red juice can often be seen dribbling down the chins of users. It often stains teeth black due to the polyphenol in the nut and leaf, which is considered attractive. The origin of the substance lies in Vietnamese legend and its use is found at weddings where a betel quid (a combination of powdered betel nut, betel leaves, lime and other flavourings) is laid out for guests. The areca nut is also a customary wedding gift given to the bride's family by the bridegroom's family. Betel and areca nuts are also presented at Tet (Lunar New Year).

building on the site today is not old. The roof can be seen from the road and in addition to the normal dragons are some curious models of what appear to be miniature Chinese landscapes carried by bowed men. Inside it is less busy than the first Thien Hau temple but on good days worshippers hurry from one image of Thien Hau (depicted here with a black face) to another waving burning joss sticks in front of her. Whatever happens in these temples is not religious in the sense of worshipping a god but more a superstition, entreating the spirits for good fortune (hence the lottery ticket sellers outside) or asking them to stave off bad luck. Note that these are not pagodas in the sense that they are not a place for the worship of Buddha and you will see no Buddhist monks here and have no sense of serene or enlightened calm. This temple has some nicely carved stone pillars of entwined dragons and on the wall to the right of the altars is a frieze of a boat being swamped by a tsunami. The walls are festooned with calendars from local Chinese restaurants and gold shops.

Ming Dynasty Assembly Hall
① *380 Tran Hung Dao St.*

The Ming Dynasty Assembly Hall (Dinh Minh Huong Gia Thanh) was built by the Cantonese community which arrived in Saigon via Hoi An in the 18th century. The assembly hall was built in 1789 to the dedication and worship of the Ming Dynasty although the building we see today dates largely from an extensive renovation carried out in the 1960s. There is some old furniture, a heavy-marble topped table and chairs which arrived in 1850 from China. It appears that the Vietnamese Emperor Gia Long used the Chinese community for cordial relations with the Chinese royal court and one of the community, a man called Trinh Hoai Duc was appointed Vietnamese ambassador to the Middle Dynasty. In the main hall there are three altars which, following imperial tradition, are: the central altar dedicated to the royal family (Ming Dynasty in this case), the right-hand altar dedicated to two mandarin officers (military) and the left-hand altar dedicated to two mandarin officers (civil).

The hall behind is dedicated to the memory of the Vuong family who built the hall and whose descendants have lived here ever since. The custodian is in fact the third generation of this family and he will explain the complexities in broken English or polished French. There is, in addition, a small side chapel where childless women can seek divine intercession from a local deity, Ba Me Sanh.

Quan Am Pagoda

ⓘ *12 Lao Tu St (just off Luong Nhu Hoc St).*

The Quan Am Pagoda is thought to be one of the oldest in the city. Its roof supports four sets of impressive mosaic-encrusted figures, while inside, the main building is fronted with old, gold and lacquer panels of guardian spirits. The main altar supports a seated statue of A-Pho, the Holy Mother. In front of the main altar is a white ceramic statue of Quan Am, the Goddess of Purity and Motherhood (Goddess of Mercy). The pagoda complex also contains a series of courtyards and altars dedicated to a range of deities and spirits. Outside, hawkers sell caged birds and vast quantities of incense sticks to pilgrims.

Binh Tay Market

The Binh Tay Market, sandwiched between Thap Muoi and Phan Van Khoe streets, is one of the most colourful and exciting markets in Ho Chi Minh City, with a wonderful array of noises, smells and colours. It sprawls over a large area and is contained in what looks like a rather decayed Forbidden Palace. Beware of pickpockets here. A new high-rise market – the five-storey **An Dong Market** – opened at the end of 1991 in Cholon. It was built with an investment of US$5 million from local ethnic Chinese businessmen.

Outer Ho Chi Minh City

Outer Ho Chi Minh City includes a clutch of scattered pagodas in several districts, namely Districts 3, 10, 11 and Binh Thanh. All are accessible by cyclo, moto or taxi. There's also a new museum of traditional medicine in District 10.

Phung Son Pagoda

ⓘ *A 40-min walk or 8-min motorbike ride from the Binh Tay Market, set back from the road at 1408 3 Thang 2 Blvd.*

The Phung Son Pagoda, also known as **Go Pagoda**, was built at the beginning of the 19th century on the site of an earlier Cambodian structure and has been rebuilt several times. At one time, it was decided to move the pagoda, and all the temple valuables were loaded on to the back of a white elephant. The beast stumbled and the valuables tumbled out into the pond that surrounds the temple. This was taken as a sign from the gods that the pagoda was to stay where it was. In the sanctuary, there is a large, seated, gilded Buddha, surrounded by a variety of other figures from several Asian and Southeast Asian countries. This, being a pagoda, has a very different atmosphere from the temples of Chinatown. There is no frenzied scrum in front of the altars and only a few whisps of smoke. Monks sit in contemplation.

Giac Vien Pagoda

ⓘ *At the end of a narrow and rather seedy 400-m-long alley running off Lac Long Quan St (just after No 247). There is a also a temple down here of no interest whatsoever, the pagoda is right at the end.*

Giac Vien Pagoda (Buddha's Complete Enlightenment) is similar in layout, content and inspiration to Giac Lam Pagoda (see below). Visiting just one of the two pagodas would be enough for most visitors. The Giac Vien Pagoda was built in 1771 and dedicated to the worship of the Emperor Gia Long. Although restored, Giac Vien remains one of the best-preserved temples in Vietnam. It is lavishly decorated, with more than 100 carvings of various divinities and spirits, dominated by a large gilded image of the Buddha of the Past (Amitabha or *A Di Da Phat* in Vietnamese). It is everything a pagoda should be: demons and gods jump out around every corner, a confusion of fantastic characters. With the smoke and smells, the richness of colour and the darkness, it's an assault on the senses. Among the decorations, note the 'Buddha lamp', funerary tablets and urns with photographs of the deceased. Outside there is a small pavilion in which the ashes of the dead are stored in small urns.

Giac Lam Pagoda

ⓘ *118 Lac Long Quan St, Ward 10, Q Tan Binh, T8-865 3933, about 2 km northeast of Giac Vien Pagoda, through an arch and down a short track about 300 m from the intersection with Le Dai Hanh St. Near the intersection is a modern 7-storey tower and beyond a giant Buddha statue which is also modern. Daily 0500-1200, 1400-2100.*

The Giac Lam Pagoda (Forest of Enlightenment) was built in 1744 and is the oldest pagoda in Ho Chi Minh City. There is a sacred Bodhi tree in the temple courtyard and the pagoda is set among fruit trees and vegetable plots. Inside Giac Lam it feels, initially, like a rather cluttered private house. In one section, there are rows of funerary tablets with pictures of the deceased – a rather moving display of man's mortality. The main altar is impressive, with layers of Buddhas, dominated by the gilded form of the Buddha of the Past. Note the 49-Buddha oil lamp with little scraps of paper tucked in. On these scraps are the names of the mourned. The number seven is very important in Buddhism and most towers have seven storeys. Behind the main temple in the section with the funerary tablets is a bust of Ho Chi Minh. At the very back of the pagoda is a hall with murals showing scenes of torture from hell. Each sin is punished in a very specific and appropriate way. The monks are very friendly and will probably offer tea. Some speak good English and French as well as having detailed knowledge of the history of the pagoda. It is a small haven of peace. An unusual feature is the use of blue and white porcelain plates to decorate the roof and some of the small towers in the garden facing the pagoda. These towers are the burial places of former head monks.

Phuoc Hai Tu (Emperor of Jade Pagoda) and around

ⓘ *73 Mai Thi Luu St off Dien Bien Phu St, 0700-1800.*

The Phuoc Hai Tu can be found, nestling behind low pink walls, just before the Thi Nghe Channel. Women sell birds that are set free to gain merit, and a pond to the right contains large turtles. The Emperor of Jade is the supreme god of the Taoists, although this temple, built in 1900, contains a wide range of other deities. These include the archangel Michael of the Buddhists, a Sakyamuni (historic) Buddha, statues of the two generals who tamed the Green Dragon (representing the east) and the White Dragon (representing the west), to the left and right of the first altar respectively, and Quan Am. The Hall of Ten Hells in the left-hand sanctuary has reliefs depicting the 1000 tortures of hell.

Nearby, the architecturally interesting **city library** ⓘ *3 Nguyen Dinh Chieu*, has a cool, modern façade; there is a memorial at the front of the building.

Tran Hung Dao Temple

ⓘ *Near the Emperor of Jade Pagoda at 34 Vo Thi Sau St, daily 0700-1100, 1430-1700.*

The small Tran Hung Dao Temple, built in 1932, was dedicated to the worship of the victorious 13th-century General Hung Dao and contains a series of bas-reliefs depicting the general's successes, along with weapons and carved dragons. In the front courtyard is a larger-than-life bronze statue of this hero of Vietnamese nationalism.

Vinh Nghiem Pagoda

ⓘ *To the west, on Nguyen Van Troi St, and just to the south of the Thi Nghe Channel.*
Another modern pagoda, the Vinh Nghiem Pagoda, was completed in 1967 and is one of the largest in Vietnam. Built in the Japanese style, it displays a classic seven-storey pagoda in a large and airy sanctuary. On either side of the entrance are two fearsome warriors; inside is a large Japanese-style Buddha in an attitude of meditation, flanked by two goddesses. Along the walls are a series of scrolls depicting the *jataka* tales, with rather quaint (and difficult to interpret) explanations in English.

Tomb and Temple of Marshal Le Van Duyet

ⓘ *126 Dinh Tien Hoang St, a 10- to 15-min cyclo ride across the Thi Nghe Channel and almost into the suburbs, 0500-1800.*
Le Van Duyet was a highly respected Vietnamese soldier who put down the Tay Son Rebellion and who died in 1831. The pagoda was renovated in 1937 – a plaque on the left lists those who made donations to the renovation fund. The main sanctuary contains a weird assortment of objects: a stuffed tiger, a miniature mountain, whale baleen, spears and other weapons of war. Much of the collection is made up of the Marshal's personal possessions. In front of the temple is the tomb itself, surrounded by a low wall and flanked by two guardian lions and two lotus buds. The pagoda's attractive roof is best seen from the tomb.

Museum of Vietnamese Traditional Medicine

ⓘ *41 Hoang Du Khuong St, District 10, T8-386 42430, www.fitomuseum.com.vn, open daily 0830-1730.*
A fascinating exploration into traditional medicine with 3000 exhibits including instruments, manuscripts, ceramic jars and model of a 19th-century pharmacy.

Around Ho Chi Minh City

Unlike Hanoi, which is so rich in sights to visit on a day out, the Ho Chi Minh City region is woefully under-endowed. The **Cu Chi Tunnels** are the most popular day trip, followed closely by an excursion to the Mekong Delta, especially **My Tho** (see page 354). It is possible to get to the coast and back in a day, **Vung Tau** (see page 289), **Long Hai** (see page 292) and **Ho Coc** (see page 293) being the obvious candidates. Ho Chi Minh City does, on the other hand, have several out-of-town sports facilities with three **golf courses** and the exhilarating **Saigon Water Park** all within less than an hour's drive (see page 60).

Cu Chi Tunnels

ⓘ *Most visitors reach Cu Chi on a tour or charter a car and include a visit to Tay Ninh – see below. Regular buses leave for Cu Chi town from the Mien Tay station (Cholon) and the Ham Nghi station; from Cu Chi it is necessary to take a Honda ôm to the tunnels or the infrequent Ben Suc bus, 10 km. It is also possible to take a motorbike from Ho Chi Minh City and back but the road (now the Bangkok to Ho Chi Minh City highway) is becoming increasingly dangerous with fast and heavy traffic. Go up Cach Mang Thang Tam St, which turns into Highway 22. Continue to Cu Chi. Go over the flyover and take the next turning to the right which is signed to the Cu Chi Tunnels. From here the tunnels are quite badly signed and you will almost certainly need to ask. Daily 0700-1630, 75,000d.*
Cu Chi Tunnels are about 40 km northwest of Ho Chi Minh City. Cu Chi town is on the main road to Tay Ninh and the Cao Dai temple and both the tunnels and the temple

can be visited in a single day trip. Dug by the Viet Minh, who began work in 1948, they were later expanded by the People's Liberation Armed Forces (PLAF, or Viet Cong) and used for storage and refuge, and contained sleeping quarters, hospitals and schools. Between 1960 and 1970, 200 km of tunnels were built. At the height of their usage, some 300,000 were living underground. The width of the tunnel entry at ground level was 22 cm by 30 cm. The tunnels are too narrow for most Westerners, but a short section of the 250 km of tunnels has been especially widened to allow tourists to share the experience. Tall or large people might still find it a claustrophobic squeeze.

Cu Chi was one of the most fervently communist of the districts around Ho Chi Minh City and the tunnels were used as the base from which the PLAF mounted the operations of the Tet Offensive in 1968. Communist cadres were active in this area of rubber plantations, even before the Second World War. Vann and Ramsey, two American soldiers, were to notice the difference between this area and other parts of the south in the early 1960s: "No children laughed and shouted for gum and candy in these hamlets. Everyone, adult and child, had a cold look" (*A Bright Shining Lie*, Sheehan 1989).

When the Americans first discovered this underground base on their doorstep (Dong Du GI base was nearby) they would simply pump CS gas down the tunnel openings and then set explosives. They also pumped river water in and used German Shepherd dogs to smell out air holes. The VC, however, smothered the holes in garlic to deter the dogs. They also used cotton from the cotton tree – kapok – to stifle the smoke from cooking; 40,000 VC were killed in the tunnels in 10 years. Later, realizing that the tunnels might also yield valuable intelligence, volunteer 'tunnel rats' were sent into the earth to capture prisoners.

Cu Chi district was a free-fire zone and was assaulted using the full battery of ecological warfare. Defoliants were sprayed and 20 tonne Rome Ploughs carved up the area in the search for tunnels. It was said that even a crow flying over Cu Chi district had to carry its own lunch. Later it was also carpet bombed with 50,000 tonnes dropped on the area in 10 years.

At **Cu Chi 1** (Ben Dinh) ⓘ *75,000d*, visitors are shown a somewhat antique but nevertheless interesting film of the tunnels during the war before being taken into the tunnels and seeing some of the rooms and the booby traps the GIs encountered. The VC survived on just cassava for up to three months and at both places you will be invited to taste some dipped in salt, sesame, sugar and peanuts. You will also be invited to a firing range to try your hand with ancient AK47s at a buck a bang.

Cu Chi 2 (Ben Duoc), has a temple, the **Ben Duoc Temple**, in memory of the 50,000 Saigon dead; the exterior is covered in mosaic murals. It stands in front of a rather beautiful sculpture of a tear called *Symbol of the Country's Spiritual Soul*.

Near the tunnels is the Cu Chi graveyard for patriots with 8000 graves. It has a very interesting large and striking bas-relief of war images along the perimeter of the entrance to the cemetery.

Cao Dai Great Temple

ⓘ *Ceremonies are held each day at 0600, 1200, 1800 and 2400, visitors can watch from the cathedral's balcony. Visitors should not enter the central portion of the nave – keep to the side aisles – and also should not wander in and out during services. If you go in at the beginning of the service you should stay until the end (1 hr). Photography is allowed. Take a tour, or charter a car in Ho Chi Minh City. Regular buses leave for Tay Ninh, via Cu Chi, from Mien Tay station (2½ hrs) or motorbike.*

Tay Ninh, the home of the temple, is 96 km northwest of Ho Chi Minh City and 64 km further on from Cu Chi town. It can be visited on a day trip from the city and can easily be combined with a visit to the Cu Chi tunnels. The idiosyncratic Cao Dai Great Temple, the 'cathedral' of the Cao Dai religion, is the main reason to visit the town.

The Cao Dai Great Temple, built in 1880, is set within a very large complex of schools and administrative buildings, all washed in pastel yellow. The twin-towered cathedral is European in inspiration but with distinct oriental features. On the façade are figures of Cao Dai saints in high relief and at the entrance is a painting depicting Victor Hugo flanked by the Vietnamese poet Nguyen Binh Khiem and the Chinese nationalist Sun Yat Sen. The latter holds an inkstone, symbolizing, strangely, the link between Confucianism and Christianity. Novelist Graham Greene in *The Quiet American* called it "The Walt Disney Fantasia of the East". Monsieur Ferry, an acquaintance of Norman Lewis, described the cathedral in even more outlandish terms, saying it "looked like a fantasy from the brain of Disney, and all the faiths of the Orient had been ransacked to create the pompous ritual…". Lewis himself was clearly unimpressed with the structure and the religion, writing in *A Dragon Apparent* that "This cathedral must be the most outrageously vulgar building ever to have been erected with serious intent".

After removing shoes and hats, women enter the cathedral through a door to the left, men to the right, and they then proceed down their respective aisles towards the altar, usually accompanied by a Cao Dai priest dressed in white with a black turban. During services they don red, blue and yellow robes signifying Confucianism, Taoism and Buddhism respectively. The men in coloured robes sporting an embroidered divine eye on their costumes are more senior. During services, on the balcony at the back of the cathedral, a group of men play a stringed instrument called a Dan Co between their feet using a bow; women sing as they play.

Two rows of pink pillars entwined with green dragons line the nave, leading up to the main altar which supports a large globe on which is painted a single staring eye – the divine, all-seeing-eye. The roof is blue and dotted with clouds, representing the heavens, and the walls are pierced by open, lattice-work windows with the divine eye as the centrepiece to the window design. At the back of the cathedral is a sculpture of Pham Com Tac, the last pope and one of the religion's founders who died in 1957. He stands on flowers surrounded by huge brown snakes and is flanked by his two assistants; one is the leader of spirits, the other the leader of materialism.

There are nine columns and nine steps to the cathedral representing the nine steps to heaven. Above the altar is the Cao Dai pantheon: at the top in the centre is Sakyamuni Buddha. Next to him on the left is Lao Tzu, master of Taosim. Left of Lao Tzu, is Quan Am, Goddess of Mercy, sitting on a lotus blossom. On the other side of the Buddha statue is Confucius. Right of the sage is the red-faced Chinese God of War and Soldiers, Quan Cong. Below Sakyamuni Buddha is the poet and leader of the Chinese saints, Li Ti Pei. Below him is Jesus and below Christ is Jiang Zhia, master of Geniism.

About 500 m from the cathedral (turn right when facing the main façade) is the **Doan Ket**, a formal garden.

The town of Tay Ninh also has a good **market** and some **Cham temples** 1 km to the southwest of the town.

Black Lady Mountain (Nui Ba Den)

① *Buses go from the bus station on Cach Mang Tam Tang St by the western edge of Tan Son Nhat Airport. From Tay Ninh to Nui Ba Den go by* Honda ôm. *There is now a cable car to the summit.*
Also known as *Nui Ba Den*, Black Lady Mountain is 10 km to the northeast of Tay Ninh and 106 km from Ho Chi Minh City. The peak rises dramatically from the plain to a height

of almost 1000 m and can be seen in the distance, to the right, on entering Tay Ninh. The Black Lady was a certain Ly Thi Huong who, while her lover was bravely fighting the occupying forces, was ordered to marry the son of a local mandarin. Rather than complying, she threw herself from the mountain. Another version of this story is that she was kidnapped by local scoundrels. A number of shrines to the Black Woman are located on the mountain, and pilgrims still visit the site. Fierce battles were also fought here between the French and Americans, and the Viet Minh. There are excellent views of the surrounding plain from the summit.

Border crossings to Cambodia
The province of Tay Ninh borders Cambodia and, before the 17th century, was part of the Khmer Kingdom. Between 1975 and December 1978, soldiers of Pol Pot's Khmer Rouge periodically attacked villages in this province, killing the men and raping the women. Ostensibly, it was in order to stop these incursions that the Vietnamese army invaded Cambodia on Christmas Day 1978, taking Phnom Penh by January 1979.

Travellers taking the bus to Phnom Penh from Ho Chi Minh City cross at **Moc Bai** (Bavet in Cambodia). Cambodian visas are available at the border; Vietnamese visas are not. There is also an underutilised crossing at **Xa Mát** in Tay Ninh Province (Trapeang Phlong) in Cambodia. Neither visas are available at the border.

Ho Chi Minh City listings

For Sleeping and Eating price codes and other relevant information, see pages 10-13.

😴 Sleeping

City centre *p24, maps p27, p29 and p35*

$$$$ Caravelle, 19 Lam Son Sq, T8-3823 4999, www.caravellehotel.com. Central and one of HCMC's top hotels. It incorporates the old **Air France Caravelle** hotel onto which it added a modern tower in 1998 and this gives it an attractive historical dimension. Very comfortable with 335 rooms, fitted out with all the mod cons, many with incredible views and well-trained and friendly staff. Breakfast is sumptuous and filling and **Restaurant Nineteen**, see page 49, serves a fantastic buffet lunch and dinner. **Saigon Saigon**, see page 55, the roof-top bar, draws the crowds until the early hours. A suite of boutique shops plus a pool and Qi Spa complete the luxury experience.

$$$$ Duxton, 63 Nguyen Hue Blvd, T8-3822 2999, www.duxton.com.au The **Duxton** is a very attractively appointed and well-finished hotel and popular with Japanese visitors. It has 198 finely decorated rooms, health club, pool and a restaurant and is well located in the heart of downtown.

$$$$ Grand, 8 Dong Khoi St, T8-3823 0163, www.grandhotel.vn. A 1930s building in the heart of the shopping district that might look more comfortable on Brighton's seafront than in HCMC. It was renovated 10 years ago but the stained glass and marble staircase have largely survived the process. A huge, modern featureless wing has been added. Lovely pool (try to get a poolside room) and a very reasonably priced restaurant. It is to be upgraded to 5 stars in 2011 with a major expansion underway.

$$$$ Hotel Catina Saigon, 109 Dong Khoi St, T8-3829 6296, www.hotelcatina.com.vn. This newcomer is brilliantly positioned on Dong Khoi with lovely, light rooms.

$$$$ Legend, 2A-4A Ton Duc Thang St, T8-3823 3333, www.legendsaigon.com. The hotel boasts HCMC's most opulent foyer. Popular with businessmen, it overlooks the river and offers a full range of restaurants, business facilities, a pool and health club. A very fine hotel with 283 rooms.

$$$$ Majestic, 1 Dong Khoi St, T8-3829 5517, www.majesticsaigon.com. Built in 1925, the hotel has character and charm and has been tastefully restored and expanded. There's a restaurant and small but nicely shaded pool. More expensive and large rooms have superb views over the river (quieter rooms at the back have pool view); from the new **M Bar** on the top floor there are magnificent views of the riverfront, especially at night.

$$$$ New World, 76 Le Lai St, T8-3822 8888, www.newworldsaigon.com. Over the years this has proved the most popular hotel with visiting businessmen. It has efficient, friendly English-speaking staff, a large attractive pool and gym and good business facilities. There are 538 guestrooms, Chinese and Western restaurants, nightclub, patisserie and bakery, dry-cleaning service and ATM. The Executive Floor offers excellent value with breakfast, afternoon tea and refreshments available all day.

$$$$ Park Hyatt Saigon, 2 Lam Son Sq, T8-3824 1234, www.saigon.park.hyatt.com. This striking hotel is in a class of its own. It exudes elegance and style and its location north of the Opera House is unrivalled. Works of art are hung in the lobby, rooms are classically furnished in French colonial style but with modern touches; the pool area is lovely; the wonderful lounge area features a baby grand piano and there are a number of very good restaurants that incorporate jaw-dropping displays of floor-to-ceiling wines in a glass display. **Square One**, see page 49, is an excellent restaurant with open kitchens and displays. There's also a fitness centre and spa.

$$$$ Renaissance Riverside, 8-15 Ton Duc Thang St, T8-3822 0033, www.marriott.com. Despite its 21 floors and 319 rooms and suites this is, in style and feel, almost a boutique hotel. Very well run, comfortable and popular with its customers. It also has Vietnam's highest atrium. Several excellent restaurants including **Kabin** Chinese restaurant and attractive pool. Executive floors provide breakfast and all-day snacks.

$$$$ Rex, 141 Nguyen Hue Blvd, T8-3829 2185, www.rexhotelvietnam.com. A historically important hotel in the heart of HCMC with unusual interior decor and a new fabulous side extension that has become the principal entrance. The original lobby is decorated entirely in wood, furnished with numerous wicker chairs, and dominated by the ceiling, a vast replica of a Dongson Drum, while the new wing is a vast cathedral of glass and marble New wing premium rooms are very smart; the Governor's Suite has a unique view of City Hall. Cheaper 'Superior' rooms in the old wing have small bathtub and are interior facing. 'Deluxe' rooms are double the size but those on the main road are noisy. Interior deluxe do not enjoy private balconies. There's a small rooftop pool awkwardly accessed through the rooftop terrace bar that's a regular pull. The new extension has created an attractive interior patio garden, the **Rose Garden**, with an open kitchen. It's a real draw and escapes the street noise.

$$$$ Saigon, 41-47 Dong Du St, T8-3829 9734, www.saigonhotel.com.vn. Opposite the mosque in a good central location. Some rooms are a bit dark and small, but it's popular and clean.

$$$$ Sheraton, 88 Dong Khoi St, T8-3827 2828, www.sheraton.com/saigon. This tall, glass-clad hotel has certainly proved popular since it opened in late 2003. There is very good lunch and dinner on offer at the **Saigon Café**, and **Level 23**, with its brilliant views across HCMC, is recommended for a night-time drink. The hotel, with modern, stylish rooms is sandwiched into a downtown street and boasts boutique shops, a gorgeous pool, a spa and tennis courts.

$$$$ Sofitel Plaza Saigon, 17 Le Duan St, T8-3824 1555, www.sofitel.com. A smart, fashionable and comfortable hotel with a delicious roof-top pool surrounded by frangipani plants. Superior rooms aren't too big but bathrooms are attractive. **L'Olivier** is a good restaurant.

$$$$-$$$ Bong Sen, 117-123 Dong Khoi St, T8-3829 1516, www.hotelbongsen.com. A **Saigontourist** well-run and upgraded hotel in a perfect location in the heart of the shopping district. It is very good value for the location but standard rooms are very small. All superior rooms have bathtubs. Few rooms have views. There is a restaurant and the **Green Leaf** café.

$$$$-$$$ Continental, 132-134, Dong Khoi St, T8-3829 9201, www.continentalhotel.com.vn. Built in 1880 and renovated in 1989, the **Continental** has an air of faded colonial splendour and its large but still-dated rooms need upgrading. The exterior has had a lick of paint. (A US$10 million renovation has been approved.) The hotel has a couple of restaurants, a business centre, fitness room and a pool. Probably in an attempt to stamp out the theft of souvenirs, you can purchase every item in the room. Don't opt for the balconied rooms overlooking Lam Son Square if you value your sleep.

$$$$-$$$ Huong Sen, 66-70 Dong Khoi St, T8-3829 1415, www.huongsenhotel.com.vn. This central hotel is popular with tour groups and good value on this street. A roof-top bar on the 7th floor is a nice place for a beer.

$$$$-$$$ Lavender Hotel, 208-210 Le Thanh Ton St, T8-2222 8888, www.lavenderhotel.com.vn. In an excellent location. The standard rooms are small but nicely furnished so you may want to opt for a superior. Helpful staff. Internet access and breakfast included.

$$$$-$$$ Palace, 56-66 Nguyen Hue Blvd, T8-3829 2860, www.palacesaigon.

com. **Saigontourist**-run hotel with some decent-sized rooms. It's very central with a restaurant and small roof-top pool.

$$$ Asian, 150 Dong Khoi St, T8-3829 6979, asianhotel@hcm.fpt.vn. Rooms with a/c and satellite TV are a little small. There's a restaurant and breakfast and Wi-Fi is included. The location is central.

$$$ Bong Sen Hotel Annex, 61-63 Hai Ba Trung St, T8-3823 5818, www.hotelbongsen. com. Sister hotel of the **Bong Sen**, this is a well-managed hotel with standard a/c rooms and a restaurant.

$$$-$$ Ho Sen, 4B-4C Thi Sach St, T8-3823 2281, www.hosenhotel.com.vn. This bland-looking hotel in a very central location is a good find. Rooms are very quiet, fairly spacious and comfortable with TVs. Staff are friendly and helpful and will store luggage.

$$$-$$ Orchid, 29A Thai Van Lung St, T8-3823 1809, www.orchid-hotel.com. In a good, central spot, surrounded by restaurants and bars, worth taking a look at. Rooms have a/c and satellite TV. Discounts for longer stays.

$$$-$$ Spring, 44-46 Le Thanh Ton St, T8-3829 7362, www.springhotelvietnam. com. Central, comfortable, charming and helpful staff; book well in advance if you want to stay in this well-run family hotel that is excellent value; breakfast included. Recommended.

$$$-$$ Tan Hai Long 3, 65 Ho Tung Mau St, T8-3915 1888, www.thlhotelgroup.com. A well-positioned hotel with small rooms, good-sized bathrooms and good service. However, check the a/c unit in your room for noise before choosing.

$$ A&EM Hotel, 60 Le Thanh Ton St, T8-3825 8529, www.a-emhotels.com. These are trying to be boutique hotels and there are flourishes but some rooms are a tad scruffy around the edges. Offers standards and deluxe – the difference being that the standards have no computer and no bathtub and no room to swing a cat. Opt for the much bigger deluxes. This **A&EM** is in a great location

$$ Khach San 69, 69 Hai Ba Trung St, T8-3829 1513, hotel69haibatrung@yahoo.com. vn. Central location with clean a/c rooms that back onto HCMC's Indian mosque. It's an ancient hotel but spotless and staff are super polite. Possibly the cheapest accommodation in the heart of downtown.

Pham Ngu Lao *p35*

$$$$-$$$ Que Huong (Liberty 4), 265 Pham Ngu Lao St, T8-3836 4556, www.libertyhotels.com.vn. A perfectly comfortable hotel. It has had to moderate its prices which means it is now possibly fair value but priced way too high for this area. Breakfast is included.

$$$$-$$$ Que Huong (Liberty 3), 187 Pham Ngu Lao St, T8-3836 9522, www. libertyhotels.com.vn. Less popular with travellers than previously as there is now more choice; cheapest rooms are on the upper floors; rather noisy.

$$$-$$ Beautiful Saigon, 62 Bui Vien St, T8-3836 4852, www.beautifulsaigonhotel. com. A new addition to the backpacker zone replacing an old hotel, this is more for the flashpackers and welcome it is too. Very nice smart and tidy rooms all with mod cons, Wi-Fi and breakfast at fair prices and recommended by happy guests.

$$-$ Hong Hoa, 185/28 Pham Ngu Lao St, T8-3836 1915, www.honghoavn.com. A well-run family hotel with 9 rooms, all a/c, hot water and private bathroom. Conveniently, the downstairs has banks of free email terminals and a supermarket.

$ Hotel Madame Cuc, 64 Bui Vien St, T8-3836 5073, 127 Cong Quynh St, T8-3836 8761, and 184 Cong Quynh St, T8-3836 1679, www.madamcuchotels.com. The reception staff at No 64 could be a lot friendlier. Rooms are quite small but the US$20 room is the bargain of the place.

$ Linh, 40/10 Bui Vien St, T8-3836 9641, hotelinh@hotmail.com. A well-priced, clean, friendly, family-run hotel with a/c and hot water. Attracts some long-stay guests. Cheaper rooms have small windows.

$ Linh Thu Guesthouse, 72 Bui Vien St, T8-3836 8421, linhthu_72bv@yahoo.com.vn. Fan rooms with bathroom and some more expensive a/c rooms too. Free internet and breakfast included.

$ Mimi Guesthouse, 40/5 Bui Vien St, T8-3836 9645, mimihotel405@yahoo.fr. 10 rooms with private bathroom, a/c, TV and Wi-Fi in rooms and hot water. Motorbikes, bikes and internet.

$ Minh Chau, 75 Bui Vien St, T8-3836 7588, minhchauhotel@hcm.vnn.vn. Some a/c, hot water and private bathrooms. It is spotlessly clean and run by 2 sisters; it has been recommexnded by lone women travellers. Free internet but breakfast not included.

Apartments

Those intending to stay a month or more might consider a furnished apartment:
Lucy Hotel, 61 Do Quang Dau St, T8-3838 9636, www.lucysaigon.com. US$450-480 per month including laundry, water and internet; often full.

Cholon *p35, map p24*

Few people stay in Cholon, but it does have the best pagodas in HCMC and is only a short cyclo ride from the centre of town.
$$$-$$ Arc en Ciel (Thien Hong), 52-56 Tan Da St, Q5, T8-3855 1662. This is the best hotel in Cholon. It boasts 4 restaurants and a rooftop bar that affords views over the district. Standard rooms are carpeted with TV and minibar but do not have much of a view and the bathroom is small. Some standard rooms enjoy bathtubs, others do not. Superior rooms have adequate-sized bathrooms.

Outer Ho Chi Minh City *p39, map p24*

These hotels are a little out of the centre – around 10-30 mins' walk or a short taxi ride.
$$$$ Thao Dien Village, 195 Nguyen Van Huong St, Thao Dien Ward, Q2, T8-3744 6458, www.thaodienvillage.com. A stylish boutique hotel and spa resort in the expat enclave. Lovely to escape the hustle of downtown. Popular restaurants too.

$$$$-$$$ Equatorial, 242 Tran Binh Trong St, Q5, T8-3839 7777, www.equatorial. com. This hotel is in a rather out-of-the-way location between Cholon and downtown HCMC but there is a free shuttle at scheduled times. It is a marble-cool oasis of calm with charming staff. The 333 rooms are tastefully furnished and there are restaurants, a gym and pool.

$ Miss Loi's Guesthouse, 178/20 Co Giang St, T8-3836 7973, missloi@hcm.fpt.vn. Cheap and cheerful, well kept, some a/c, breakfast included, popular. US$300-400 per month.

🍴 Eating

HCMC has a rich culinary tradition and, as home to people from most of the world's imagined corners, its cooking is diverse. You could quite easily eat a different national cuisine every night for several weeks. French food is well represented and there are many restaurants from neighbouring Asian countries especially Japan, Korea, China and Thailand. The area between Le Thanh Ton and Hai Ba Trung streets has become a 'Little Tokyo' and 'Little Seoul' on account of the number of Japanese and Korean restaurants. HCMC, it is said, has the cheapest Japanese food in the world.

Pham Ngu Lao, the backpacker area, is chock-a-block with low-cost restaurants many of which are just as good as the more expensive places elsewhere. Do not overlook street-side stalls whose staples consist of *pho* (noodle soup), *bánh xeo* (savoury pancakes), *cha giò* (spring rolls) and *banh mi pate* (baguettes stuffed with pâté and salad), all usually fresh and very cheap. The major hotels all have gourmet shops selling bread and pastries. Eating out is an informal business; suits are not necessary anywhere, and in Pham Ngu Lao expect shorts and sandals.

The Ben Thanh night market (see page 33) is a major draw for Vietnamese and overseas visitors. Stalls are set up at dusk and traffic suppressed. There is a good range of inexpensive foodstall dishes and lots of noodles; it stays open until around 2300.

City centre *p24, maps p27, p29 and p35*

An Vien, 178A Hai Ba Trung St, T8-3824 3877. Open 1200-2300. This excellent and intimate restaurant is on 3 floors. Each room is small and furnished in Vietnamese style. The food – Vietnamese – is excellent; it serves some of the most fragrant rice in Vietnam. Service is attentive but discreet.

Dynasty, New World Hotel, see Sleeping, page 45, T8-3822 8888. A long Chinese menu and excellent lunchtime dim sun.

Hoi An, 11 Le Thanh Ton St, T8-3823 7694. Open 1730-2300. This is a sister (and almost neighbouring) restaurant of **Mandarin** (see below). The building is a good replica of a Hoi An house, a theme that is repeated in the decor and staff uniforms. Service and food (Vietnamese) are good although the clientele are mostly tourists, so do not expect good value for money.

Kabin, Renaissance Riverside Hotel, see Sleeping, page 44, T8-3822 0033. One of HCMC's best Chinese restaurants; it sometimes features chefs from China.

Mandarin, 11A Ngo Van Nam St, T8-3822 9783. Open 1130-1400, 1730-2300. One of the finest restaurants in HCMC serving up a culinary mix of exquisite flavours from across the country amid elegant decor including stunning, richly coloured silk tablecloths. The food is delicious but it's not very Vietnamese and the service is a little over the top.

Maxim's Nam An, 13-17 Dong Khoi St, T8-3829 6676. Open 1000-2300. Massive menu; the food receives mixed reviews but the floorshows at 2000 are widely acclaimed and reservations are wise.

Qucina, 7 Lam Son Sq, T8-3824 6325. Mon-Sat 1800-2300. Smart and stylish Italian restaurant serving divine cuisine. It's attached to the popular **Q Bar** under the Opera House.

Square One, Park Hyatt Saigon, 2 Lam Son Sq, T8-3824 1234. Open1200-1430, 1800-2230. Charming, efficient and friendly staff manage an extensive menu of Vietnamese seafood. Sit out or in among the gorgeous carved screens dividing the eating and cooking stations. There are 5 show kitchens – Western Grill, Vietnamese steam and woks, seafood, a dessert counter and a juice and tea area. Dine amid the fish tanks and admire the floor-to-ceiling wine bottles – 1500 perfectly stacked up. Try the Nha Trang oysters and the signature spicy rolls that are an interesting twist on an old classic; avoid the tasteless white ice cream and don't overdose on the sherbert on the dessert menu.

La Camargue, 191 Hai Ba Trung St, Q3, T8-3520 4888. Open 1800-2300. One of HCMC's longest-standing restaurants and bars it has remained consistently one of the most successful and popular places in town but it has had to move from its central French villa to one hidden further out of downtown. There's still an upstairs open-air terrace restaurant serving excellent food from an international menu with a strong French influence.

Pacharan, 97 Hai Ba Trung St, T8-3825 6024. Open 1100-late. A hit from the beginning, this Spanish restaurant is nearly full every night with happy and satisfied customers. The open-air rooftop bar that overlooks the **Park Hyatt Hotel** is a winner when there's a cool breeze blowing through the terrace. Fans of Spanish fare will love the (expensive) Iberian cured ham from rare, semi-wild acorn-fed black-footed pigs as well as staples such as anchovies, olives, mushrooms and prawns; all the tapas are beautifully presented. Don't forget to have a tipple of one of the numerous *vinos tintos* lining the wall of the bar.

Restaurant Nineteen, Caravelle Hotel, see Sleeping, page 45, T8-3823 4999. Open 1130-1430, 1745-2200. A buffet of Japanese sushi, Chinese dim sum, seafood, a range of hot dishes, cheeses and puddings galore. Weekends are especially extravagant with excellent roast beef. The free-flow of wine makes it an epicurean delight and tremendous value for money.

♥♥♥-♥♥ Temple Club, 29 Ton That Thiep St, T8-3829 9244. Open 1100-1400, 1830-2230. This is a most beautifully furnished club and restaurant open to non-members in French-colonial style and the effect is striking. Tasty Vietnamese dishes are excellent value. There's a very pleasant club area in which to meet and have a drink. The restaurant is popular so it's wise to book.

♥♥♥-♥ Zanzbar, 41 Dong Du St, T8-3822 7375. Enormous portions of surf and turf. Dine outside on the mini terrace when the heat is hotting up.

♥♥ Augustin, 10 Nguyen Thiep St, T90-866 8081. Mon-Sat 1130-1400, 1800-2230. Fairly priced and some of the best, unstuffy French cooking in HCMC; tables are pretty closely packed and there is a congenial atmosphere at this small and central restaurant. Try the excellent gratinée onion soup and baked clams.

♥♥ Blue Ginger (Saigon Times Club), 37 Nam Ky Khoi Nghia St, T8-3829 8676. Open 0700-1430 and 1700-2200. A gorgeous restaurant in style, welcome and comfort, it offers a feast of Vietnamese food for diners with more than 100 dishes on its menu. Dine indoors in the cellar-like restaurant or outdoors in a small courtyard accompanied by charming staff offering courteous and discrete service.

♥♥ Hoa Vien, 28 bis Mac Dinh Chi St, T8-3829 0585. Open 0900-2400. An amazing and vast Czech bierkeller boasting HCMC's first microbrewery. Freshly brewed dark and light beer available by the litre or in smaller measures. Grilled mackerel, pork and sausages all are very useful for soaking up the alcohol.

♥♥ Jaspas, 33 Dong Khoi St, T8-3822 9926. Open 0830-late. This welcoming restaurant in the heart of the shopping district serves up a superlative, unmissable melt-in-the-mouth raw tuna encrusted with sesame. Come back to try other tantalizingly good starters such as salt and pepper squid and goat's cheese parcels. For mains there's lamb shank, blackened barrimundi seared in cajun

spices and *spanikopita* for vegetarians. If you have any room left tuck into the apple and blueberry crumble with vanilla ice cream.

♥♥ La cantine on the 6, 6 Dong Khoi St, T8-3823 8866, www.lacantine.vn. Opt for the street-front **Cafe Bistro** for excellent people-watching opportunities and opt for the great-value express lunches or bistro dinners. English is not well spoken by staff.

♥♥ La Fourchette, 9 Ngo Duc Ke St, T8-3829 8143. Open 1200-1430, 1830-2230. A truly excellent and authentic little French bistro. Warm welcome, well-prepared dishes, generous portions and local steak as tender as any import. Booking advised. Recommended.

♥♥ Le Jardin, 31 Thai Van Lung St, T8-3825 8465. Mon-Sat 1100-1400, 1800-2100. Excellent little French café, part of the **French Cultural Institute**. Eat inside or in the garden and indulge in the good food.

♥♥ The Refinery, 74 Hai Ba Trung St, T8-3823 0509. Open 1100-2300. This former opium factory (through the arch and on the left) is a little understated in its reincarnation. The herb-encrusted steak and grilled barramundi are delicious but the seared tuna with lentil salad is outstanding. Braised rabbit and duck and apple tagine with raisin and butter couscous are other menu offerings. Admire the original fleur-de-lys tiles and photos of the working factory while you wait.

♥♥ Saigon Indian, 1st floor, 73 Mac Thi Buoi St, T8-3824 5671. Open 1115-1430, 1730-2230. Proving to be a very popular Indian restaurant it has a wide range of dishes from north and south with tandoori dishes and plenty of vegetarian options. Delicious garlic nan bread.

♥♥ Tib, 187 Hai Ba Trung St, Q3, T8-3829 7242. Open 1100-1400, 1700-2200. This is a little pocket of Hué in HCMC furnished in the dark wood so favoured by the area but is more of an Imperial lite. There's an extensive menu, which includes a good selection of Hué specialities and the food is good. The atmosphere is convivial and the restaurant, which is down an alley off the main road, is popular with Vietnamese families. The incredible wine stock is a bonus.

Wild Horse Saloon, 8A/1D1 Thai Van Lung St, T8-3825 1901, www. wildhorsesteakhouse.com. 1000-1400, 1600-2330. Unmissable with its monumental beer barrel façade, this Tex Mex (which has turned more low-key on its theme) is a popular spot for a good old Sun roast. Dine at solid wood tables on pastas, burgers, Mexican meatballs, crab cakes or Texas-style rack of lamb. The Sun roast of pork, chicken, beef or lamb is served with boiled vegetables, roast potato, gravy, stuffing, crackling and apple sauce. The separate bar area, entered by a massive, cut-out beer barrel, shows sport TV.

Al Fresco's, 27 Dong Du St, T8-3822 7317. Open 0830-1400, 1830-2300. Opened in late 2003 and sister of the famous Hanoi restaurant, it has been a huge success from its first day. The Australian-run restaurant specializes in ribs, steak, pizzas, hamburgers and Mexican dishes which are all excellent and highly popular. It serves giant portions: think before ordering the rack of ribs. Book or be prepared to wait. Delivery available.

Ashoka, 17A/10 Le Thanh Ton St, T8-3823 1372. Open 1100-1400, 1700-2230. Delicious food from an extensive menu at this beacon of Indian cuisine. Its set lunch lists 11 options with a further, extraordinary 19 curry dishes. Highlights in the low-lit, comfortably a/c restaurant are mutton *shami* kebab, prawn vindaloo and *kadhai* fish – barbecued chunks of fresh fish cooked in *kadhai* (a traditional Indian-style wok with Peshwari ground spices and sautéd with onion and tomatoes).

Hoa Tuc, 74 Hai Ba Trung St, T8-3825 1676. Open 1000-2230. A new addition to this popular courtyard dining space. Dine amid the art deco accents on soft shell crab or a salad of pink pomelo, squid and crab with herbs. The desserts are tantalizing. Try the Earl Grey tea custard. Portions a tad on the small side. Cooking classes available.

Kita, 39 Nguyen Hue St, T8-3821 5300. Open 0730-2200, Sun 0730-1600. A bright

and breezy café in a French colonial corner building serving top salads, soups, and sandwiches. Popular with the expat crowd. Try for the balconies on the upper floors.

Spice, 27C Le Quy Don St, T8-3930 7873. Open 1100-1400 and 1730-2230. This is an excellent Thai restaurant and is very popular, especially with the younger set. Prices are reasonable and the food is authentically Thai. Welcoming and friendly service and an entertaining menu with horoscopes.

Villa FB, 79 Suong Nguyet Anh St, T8-6290 6571, www.villafb.com. Open 0700-2300. This might be all style over substance in an oriental chic that is trying too hard. Raining walls of glass and choreographed black and white furniture evoke sleek Saigon but a crab dish came with real crab plus crabsticks; unforgivable. Menu options are tempting and there are few other options in this part of town stufffed with a growing number of hotels.

Warda, 71/7 Mac Thi Buoi St, T8-3823 3822, www.wardavn.com. Open Mon-Sat 0900-2400, Sun 1500-2400. A Bedouin tent huddles over plump pumpkin-coloured cushions on sofas amid a few shisha pipes at the end of this buzzy alley. The menu options are tantalizing and this is a wonderful way to break from Vietnamese menus. It's a meat-lovers paradise but vegetarians are not ignored.

13 Ngo Duc Ke, 15 Ngo Duc Ke St, T8-3823 9314. Open 0600-2230. Fresh, well cooked, honest Vietnamese fare, chicken in lemon grass (no skin, no bone) is a great favourite and the beef (*bo luc lac*) melts in the mouth. Popular with locals, expats and travellers. Vegetarians, soup lovers and squid eaters are catered for too.

Au Parc, 23 Han Thuyen St, T8-3829 2772. Open Mon-Sat 0730-2230, Sun 0800-1700. Facing on to the park in front of the old Presidential Palace this attractive café serves snacks and light meals including sandwiches, salads, juices and drinks; it also does a good Sun brunch; lovely spot for a leisurely breakfast Delivery available.

Bombay, 59 Dong Du St, T090-386 3114. Open for lunch and carries on until around 2100. Almost opposite the mosque; a long-established and informal restaurant serving excellent curries and very good paratha.

Com Nieu Saigon, 19 Tu Xuong St, Q3, T8-3932 2799. Open 1000-2200. Well known for the theatricals which accompany the serving of the speciality baked rice: one waiter smashes the earthenware pot before tossing the contents across the room to his nimble-fingered colleague standing by your table. Deserves attention for its excellent food and a good selection of soups.

Hoang Yen, 5-7 Ngo Duc Ke St, T8-3823 1101. Open 1000-2200. Utterly plain setting and decor but absolutely fabulous Vietnamese dishes, as the throngs of local lunchtime customers testify. Soups and chicken dishes are ravishing.

Indian Curry-Rice Restaurant, 66 Dong Du St, T8-3823 2159. Open 1000-2000. A small, canteen-like restaurant behind the down-town mosque. Enter the compound and walk to the right and around the back. The aroma will greet you before you see the superb spread of vegetarian and meat curries and stuffed bread – pots, pans and stoves all on view. A curry extravangaza of chicken, fish, goat, beef, cuttlefish, shrimp and crab served with yellow rice by the very friendly staff will provide a filling meal.

Juice, 49 Mac Thi Buoi St, T8-3829 6900. Open 0730-2200. Hidden away in a tiny outlet, **Juice** offers dozens of scrummy options from sandwiches, bagels and paninis (and more types of bread) to healthy smoothies. Its modern comfy seating, attentive staff and large portions attract working expats and Vietnamese for lunchtime meetings.

Mogambo, 50 Pasteur St, T8-3825 1311. Open 0730-2300. The bar and restaurant serves cold beer, excellent burgers, steaks, pies and fries. Popular with American expats and now in a new location.

Pho 24, 71-73 Dong Khoi St, www.pho24. com.vn. Convenient and quick pho from this noodle soup chain.

Pho Hoa Pasteur, 260C Pasteur St. Open 0600-2400. Probably the best known of all *pho* restaurants and packed with customers and dizzying aromas. The *pho*, which is good, and costs more than average comes in 10 options and is served in the small restaurant with tables tightly arranged. Chinese bread and wedding cake (*banh xu xe*) provide the only alternative in this specialist restaurant.

Wrap & Roll, 62 Hai Ba Trung St, T8-3822 2166. Open 0730-2230. This is the Vietnamese equivalent of a **Wagamama's**. It has a plethora of options at bargain prices including wrap your own spring rolls, *banh xeo*, soups, desserts and smoothies. The mint-green walls match the modern finish; the branding, prices and substance is pulling in the punters – young Vietnamese and expats alike.

Cafés, bakeries and foodstalls

Cooku'nest Café, 13 Tu Xuong St, Q3, T8-2241 2043. This kooky venue looks like it has been hoiked off an Alpine slope. It's a pine cabin equipped with cuckoo clock. Sit upstairs on the floor next to tiny tables and mingle with the local student gang. There's live music every night. Wi-Fi available.

La Fenêtre Soleil, 2nd floor, 135 Le Thanh Ton St (entrance at 125 Nam Ky Khoi Nghia St), T8-3822 5209. Open Mon-Sat, café 0900-1900, bar 1900-2400. Don't be put off by the slightly grimy side entrance; clamber up into the boho-Indochine world of this gorgeous café/bar, artfully cluttered with antiques, lamps, comfy sofas and home-made cakes, muffins, smoothies and other delights. The high-energy drinks of mint, passionfruit, and ginger juice are lovely. Highly recommended.

Kem Bach Dang, 26-28 Le Loi Blvd. On opposite corners of Pasteur St. A very popular café serving fruit juice, shakes and ice cream. Try the coconut ice cream (*kem dua*) served in a coconut.

Tous les Jours, 180 Hai Ba Trung St, Q3, and also in several other locations including

Diamond Plaza, T8-3823 8302. Open 0600-2300. A smorgasbord of cakes and pastries awaits the hungry visitor.

Pham Ngu Lao *p35*

Nearly all these restaurants are open all day every day from early or mid-morning until 2230 or later – when the last customer leaves, as they like to say. All are geared to Westerners and their habits and tastes and in just about all of them there will be at least one person who speaks English and French. Most tend to be cheap but prices have risen in recent times; do check

†††Good Morning Vietnam, 197 De Tham St, T8-3837 1894. Open 0900-2400. One of the popular chain of Italian restaurants in southern Vietnam. Italian owned and run and serving up Italian flavours. Their pizzas are delicious and salads are good.

†Bobby Brewers Coffee, 45 Bui Vien St, Pham Ngu Lao, T8-3920 4090, www. bobbybrewers.com. Western-style coffee bar with burgers and baguettes. 5 movies a day shown too.

†Cafe Zoom, 169A De Tham St, T1222 993585, www.vietnamvespaadventure. com. Laid-back vibe and venue serving top burgers and fries.

†Cappuccino, 258 De Tham St, T8-3837 4114, and 86 Bui Vien St, T8-3920 3134. Open 0800-2300. Running since 1992, with a good range of well-prepared Italian food at sensible prices: pizzas, pasta, a very good lasagne and zabaglione. Wine by the glass – either French or Dalat wine. The Bui Vien branch is particularly good.

†Kim Café, 268 De Tham St, T8-3836 8122. Open from early till late. Wide range of food, popular with travellers and expats. One of the best-value breakfasts in the country.

†Lac Thien, 207 Bui Vien St, T090-445 6103. Open 0800-2300. Vietnamese food. This outpost of the well-known **Lac Thien** in Hué is run by the same family. *Banh xeo* (savoury pancake) is a major feature of the menu.

†Lucky or **May Man**, 224 De Tham St, T8-3836 7277. Italian food (Japanese upstairs),

bar and breakfasts. Good value and popular.

†Margherita, 175/1 Pham Ngu Lao St, T8-3837 0760. Open 0700-1300, 1500-2400. Serves good Italian at reasonable prices.

†Sozo, 176 Bui Vien, T8-6271 9176, www. sozocentre.com. As well as coffees of every shade, this place serves bagels, and excellent cookies with proceeds going to charity.

†Zen Plaza, 54-56 Nguyen Trai St, close to Pham Ngu Lao, T8-3925 0339. Open 1000-2200. Sushi lovers will want to come here for a good feed washed down by the plum wine. It is convenient for the backpacker district. The set menus are excellent value.

Cholon *p35, map p24*

The Chinese seem to prefer eating in cavernous restaurants or at street side noodle stands. Cholon has more of the latter.

†††Tien Phat, 18 Ky Hoa St, Q9, T8-3853 6217. Conveniently located near the temples of Cholon. Open for breakfast and lunch. Specializes in dim sun. A good selection of freshly prepared dim sun is nice with hot tea.

Outer Ho Chi Minh City *p39, map p24*

†††The Deck, 38 Nguyen U Di, An Phu, Q2, T8-3744 6322, www.thedecksaigon.com. A very popular expat nightspot with tables on a decking right on the Saigon River. The food, rich in meats and fish is, in the main, delicious and creative. It's an elegant spot and a big draw in the area.

†††-††Le Bordeaux, 72 D2 St, Cu Xa Van Thanh Bac, Q Binh Thanh, T8-3899 9831, www.restaurant-lebordeaux.com.vn. Mon 1830-2130, Tue-Sat 1130-1330, 1830-2130. Rather a tragedy that it is in such an awkward location. If you can find it you are in for a treat. Lovely decor and warm atmosphere, receives the highest accolades for its French cuisine but it is not cheap.

†Bo Tuong Xeo Chan May (formerly **Luong Son**) 65 Nguyen Van Sang St, Tan Nhi Ward, Tan Phu District, near the airport, T8-3812 1820. Open 0900-2200. Noisy, smoky, chaotic and usually packed, this large, restaurant that has had to move from downtown specializes in *bo tung xeo* (sliced beef barbecued at the table served with mustard sauce – the name also refers to a gruesome torture, ask Vietnamese friends for details). The beef, barbecued squid and other delicacies are superb. This restaurant is also the place to sample unusual dishes such as scorpion, porcupine, fried cricket, coconut worm and cockerel's testicles.

Foodstalls

362-376 Hai Ba Trung St, just north of Tan Dinh market. Everyone has their favourite but these restaurants serve excellent chicken rice (*com ga*), **No 381, Hong Phat**, is good. All charge just over US$2 for steamed chicken and rice (*com gà hap*) with soup.

Anh Thu, 49 Dinh Cong Trang St, and other stalls nearby on the south side of Tan Dinh market serve *cha gio, banh xeo, bi cuon* and other Vietnamese street food.

Nguyen Trai St (extreme east end of the street, by the **New World Hotel** roundabout). Late night *pho* is available from stalls in this area.

Tran Cao Van St, east of Cong Truong Quoc Te, Q3. The restaurants and stalls here serve delicious noodles of all kinds, especially noodle soup with duck (*my vit*).

Vietnamese cafés

Vietnamese tend to prefer non-alcoholic drinks and huge numbers of cafés exist to cater to this market. Young romantic couples sit in virtual darkness listening to Vietnamese love songs all too often played at a deafening volume while sipping coffee. The furniture tends to be rather small for the Western frame but these cafés are an agreeable way of relaxing after dinner in a more typically Vietnamese setting.

⏻ Bars and clubs

Along with the influx of foreigners and the freeing up of Vietnamese society has come a rapid increase in the number of bars in HCMC and they cater to just about all tastes – drink, music and company-wise. At one time hotel bars were just about the only safe and legal place for foreigners to drink but now they are beginning to look much the same as hotel bars the world over. The rooftop bar at the **Rex Hotel** is an exception.

Bar opening times can be a little difficult to predict as it depends entirely upon the whim of the local police. Some stay open until 0200-0300 but at other times the police shut them down at 2400. The **Pham Ngu Lao** area has a few bars, most have pool tables, and tend to be busy later at night and tend to stay open longer than those in the centre.

Alibi, 11 Thai Van Lung St, T8-3822 3240. Goes on after hours and is a magnet for tourists and expats. There's a small terrace to escape the inner heat.

Apocalypse Now, 2BCD Thi Sach St, T8-3825 6124. Open 2100-0300. Free admission for Westerners. Gets going after 2300 and stays open very late if the police permit. Each night crowds of tourists go in search of a legend, or in search of something. It remains one of the most popular and successful bars and clubs in HCMC and draws a very wide cross section of punters of all ages and nationalities. The crowded dancefloor gets very sticky; the ceiling is decorated with helicopter reliefs – the fans revolving as if they were the helicopter blades. There's quite a large outside area at the back where it's possible to strike up a conversation.

Blue Gecko, 31 Ly Tu Trong St, T8-3824 3483. It has been adopted by HCMC's Australian community so expect cold beer and Australian flags above the pool table.

The Cage, 3A Ton Duc Thang St. Fashionable new clubby hangout for the young and beautiful. Guest DJs spin the tunes for the city's clubbing denizens. Drinks are expensive.

Cyclo Bar, 163 Pham Ngu Lao St, T8-3920 1567. 0700-2400. A welcome addition to this neighbourhood. Inexpensive drinks and light meals from breakfast onwards.

The Hi Fi, Level 2, 38 Nguyen Hue St, www.thehifi.asia. Good central spot for catching live acts.

Le Pub, 175/22 Pham Ngu Lao St, T8-3837 7679, www.lepub.org. Like its Hanoi counterpart, a great meeting place for a beer and good slap-up nosh. You can sit out front and watch the world go by.

Lush, 2 Ly Tu Trong St, T8-3824 2496. Quite an impressive set-up for HCMC with an outdoor area for hanging, funky indoors area for drinking and a balcony for watching. There's also a pool table and when the DJs start spinning the dance floor gets packed especially on Fri and Sat.

Q Bar, 7 Lam Son Sq, under the **Opera House**, T8-3823 3479. 1800 till the small hours, police permitting. The most sophisticated of HCMC's bars with striking decor and design and haunt of a wide cross-section of HCMC society: the sophisticated, intelligent, witty, rich, handsome, cute, curvaceous, camp, glittering and famous are all to be found here. **Qucina**, Q Bar's Italian restaurant, is attached and meals can be served at the bar.

Rex Hotel Bar, see Sleeping, above. An open-air rooftop bar which has a kitsch revolving crown. There are good views, cooling breeze, snacks and meals – and a link with history.

Saigon Saigon, 10th floor of the **Caravelle Hotel**, 19 Lam Son Sq, T8-3824 3999. It is breezy and cool, has large comfortable chairs in which to loll and superb views by day and by night. Excellent cocktails but they're not cheap.

Sax n' Art, 28 Le Loi St, T8-3822 8472. Open 1700-2400. A new jazz club for the city in a central location with nightly performances. Popular with tourists and locals.

Storm-P, 28 Cao Ba Quat, T8-3822 1539. HCMC's Scandinavian bar, popular with Danes and Swedes (not to mention the odd Scot or 2). Friendly staff to chat to at the bar and a few Danish dishes for the homesick.

Vasco's, 74/7D I lai Ba Trung St, T8-3824 2888. Open 1600-2400. A hugely popular expat spot now in its new courtyard setting. **Xu Restaurant Lounge**, Level 1, 71-75 Hai Ba Trung St, T8-3824 8468, www.xusaigon.com. Excuse the strange alleyway entrance and climb the steps to this bar, which is trying for a modern London feel and is certainly an ultra-cool refuge away from the hurly-burly of downtown. However, the proximity of the restaurant and its harsh lighting is a little stark. The impossibly glamorous bar staff are friendly and some seating is more comfortable than others. Choose your drinks wisely; avoid the *sake-tinis* but the passionfruit *caprioska* slips down a treat.

In Pham Ngu Lao, the **Go2** and **Buffalo** cluster are the junction of De Tham and Bui Vien streets is always busy and for much later night jinks, move to the **T&R Tavern** on Do Quang Dau St.

Cinemas
Diamond Plaza has a cinema on the 13th floor of this shopping centre which screens English-language films.

French Cultural Institute (**Idecaf**), 31 Thai Van Lung St, T8-3829 5451, www.idecaf.gov.vn. French films are screened here.

Galaxy, 116 Nguyen Du St, T8-3823 5235, www.galaxycine.vn shows English-language movies on 3 big screens.

Traditional music and opera
Conservatory of Music (**Nhac Vien Thanh Pho Ho Chi Minh**), 112 Nguyen Du St, T8-3824 3774, www.hcmcchoir.com. Traditional Vietnamese music and classical music concerts are performed by the young students who study music here and sometimes by local and visiting musicians.

Opera House, Lam Son Sq, T8-3832 2009. Infrequent concerts are held here. Consult the *Vietnam News* and other local publications for upcoming events or visit the ticket office. Ticket prices vary. Also consult www.hbso.org.vn for the city's ballet symphony orchestra and opera.

TrucMai House, 104 Pham Viet Chanh St, Ward 19, Q Binh Thanh, T8-3840 1762, www.trucmaimusic.com. Dinh Linh and his wife Tuyet Mai perform home concerts, introduce you to the traditional instruments and allow you to try some of them. This is a very interesting and worthwhile experience. **Buffalo Tours**, www.buffalotours.com, offers this as a tour.

Water puppetry
Golden Dragon Water Puppet Theatre, 55B Nguyen Thi Minh Khai St, T8-3930 2196, www.thaiduongtheatre.com. A new 50-min performance daily at 1830 and 2000.
Museum of Vietnamese History, 2 Nguyen Binh Khiem St, T8-3829 8146, www.baotanglichsuvn.com. There are daily 15-min water puppetry performances in the tiny theatre in an outdoor, covered part of the museum, see page 32. The advantage of this performance over the Hanoi theatre is that the audience can get closer to the puppetry and there is better light and more room for manoeuvre when taking photos.

✪ Shopping

Antiques
Most shops are on **Dong Khoi, Mac Thi Buoi** and **Ngo Duc Ke** streets. For the knowledgeable, there are bargains to be found, especially Chinese and Vietnamese ceramics – however you will need an export permit to get them out of the country. Also available are old watches, colonial bric-à-brac, lacquerware and carvings, etc. For the less touristy stuff, visitors would be advised to spend an hour or so browsing the treasure trove shops in **Le Cong Trieu St** (aka **Antique St**). It runs between Nam Ky Khoi Nghia and Pho Duc Chinh streets just south of Ben Thanh Market. Among the bric-a-brac and tat are some interesting items of furniture, statuary, stamps, candlesticks, fans, badges and ceramics. Bargaining is the order of the day and some pretty good deals can be struck.

Art and gifts
HCMC has acquired something of a reputation for its galleries and a number of artists have a considerable international following. There are countless shops which do nothing but reproduce works of art and are willing to turn their hand to anything. They will produce an oil portrait from a crumpled passport photograph, paint a stately home from a postcard or a grand master from a photograph in a magazine. There is also a lot of colourful 'original' work cheaply available around **Pham Ngu Lao** and the **Dong Khoi** area.
Ancient/Apricot, 50-52 Mac Thi Buoi St, T8-3822 7962, www.apricotgallery.com.vn. This specializes in famous artists and commands high prices.
Dogma, 175 De Tham St, www.dogma. vietnam.com. Sells propaganda posters, funky T-shirts and postcards.
Duc Minh Art Gallery, 31c Le Quy Don St, Q3, T8-3933 0498, ducminh-art@hcm.vnn. vn. Daily 0900-1200, 1400-1800. A small gallery with a few interesting works. Those by Tran Long are still lifes and portraits with a photographic-like quality.
Gaya, 1 Nguyen Van Trang St, corner of Le Lai St, T8-3925 2495, www.gayavietnam. com. Open 0900-2100. A 3-storey shop with heavenly items: exquisitely embroidered tablecloths, bamboo bowls, ceramics and large home items such as screens; also gorgeous and unusual silk designer clothes by, among others, Romyda Keth, based in Cambodia. If you like an item but it does not fit they will take your measurements but it could take a fortnight to make.
Hanoi Gallery, 43 Le Loi Blvd, T098-203 8803 (mob). Like its counterpart in Hanoi it sells propaganda posters.
Lotus, 25 Dong Khoi St, T8-3824 8977. Old propaganda posters galore.
Lotus Gallery, 47 Dong Khoi St, T8-3829 2695, www.lotusgallery.com. Another expensive gallery at the top end of the market. Many are members of the Vietnam Fine Arts Association and many have exhibited around the world.

Mosaique, 98 Mac Thi Buoi St, T8-3823 4634, www.mosaiquedecoration.com. Open 0900-2100. Like its sister store in Hanoi, this boutique, which is rather like entering a cavern, is a home accessories parlour. Upstairs exquisitely embroidered wall hangings and table runners are displayed.
Nagu, 132-134 Dong Khoi St (next to the Park Hyatt), www.zantoc.com. Delicate embroidered silk products among other fashion, home and giftware.
Nguyen Freres, 2 Dong Khoi St, T8-3823 9459, www.nguyenfreres.com. An absolute Aladdin's cave. Don't miss this – even if it's just to potter among the collectable items.
Saigon Kitsch, 43 Ton That Tiep St, www. saigonkitsch.com. 0900-2000. This is the place to come for communist kitsch ranging from big propaganda art posters to placemats and mugs – there is some essential buying here for those who like this kind of thing. Also retro bags and funky jewellery on sale.

Bicycles
From the stalls along **Le Thanh Ton St** close to the Ben Thanh Market and Vo Thi Sau west of the junction with Pham Ngoc Thach St. US$40 for a Vietnamese bike, at least US$70 for a better-built Chinese one.

Books, magazines and maps
All foreigners around Pham Ngu Lao and De Tham streets are game to the numerous booksellers who hawk mountains of pirate books under their arms and stagger from table to table. The latest bestsellers together with enduring classics (ie *The Quiet American*) can be picked up for a couple of dollars.
Artbook, 43 Dong Khoi St, T8-3910 3518, www.artbookvn.com. For art, architecture and coffeetable books.
Bookazine, 28 Dong Khoi St. A decent range of English-language books.
Fahasa, 40 Nguyen Hue Blvd, T8-3912 5358, www.fahasasg.com. A very large store with dozens of English titles and magazines.

Western newspapers and magazines
Sold in the main hotels. Same day *Bangkok Post* and *The Nation* newspapers (English-language Thai papers), and up-to-date *Financial Times*, *Straits Times*, *South China Morning Post*, *Newsweek* and *The Economist*, available from larger bookshops.

Maps
HCMC has the best selection of maps in Vietnam, at stalls on Le Loi Blvd between Dong Khoi St and Nguyen Hue Blvd. Bargain hard – the bookshops are probably cheaper.

Clothing, silk and *ao dai*
Dong Khoi, with its many excellent boutiques, is the street that most Western and Japanese women head straight for. Vietnamese silk and traditional dresses (*ao dai*) are to be found in the shops on Dong Khoi St and in Ben Thanh Market. A number of shops in De Tham St sell woven and embroidered goods including bags and clothes.
Ipa Nima, 77-79 Dong Khoi St and in the New World Hotel, T8-3822 3277, www.ipa-nima.com. Sister branch of the Hanoi store with the sparkling and alluring products and must- have accessories for new seasons.
Khaisilk, 107 Dong Khoi, T8-3829 1146. Khaisilk belongs to Mr Khai's growing empire (see box, page 86). He has a dozen shops around Vietnam. Beautifully made, quality silk products from dresses to scarves to ties can be found in this luxury outlet.
Mai's, 132-134 Dong Khoi St, T8-3827 2733, www.mailam.com.vn. One of the most exciting designers working in Vietnam.
Song, 76D Le Thanh Ton St, T8-3824 6986, www.valeriegregorimckenzie.com. Open 0900-2000. A beautiful clothes emporium. It's hard to resist buying something from this shop. Lovely, flowing summer dresses from designer Valerie Gregori McKenzie plus other stylish and unique pieces plus accessories and cookbooks. Recommended.

Department stores

Diamond Department Store, Diamond Plaza 1st-4th floor, 34 Le Duan St, T8-3822 5500. Open 1000-1000. HCMC's central a/c department store set over a couple of floors. It sells luxury goods, clothes with some Western brands, watches, bags and perfumes. There is also a small supermarket inside. A bowling alley complex and cinema dominate the top floor.

Hung Vuong Plaza, 126 Hung Vuong St, Q5 is the largest department store in Vietnam.

The Opera View, 161 Dong Khoi St, corner of Le Loi. Opened in mid-2007, it houses Louis Vuitton, Burberry and the like.

Parkson Plaza, 35 Bis - 45 Le Thanh Ton St. A new high-end department store.

Foodstores

Shops specializing in Western staples such as cornflakes, peanut butter and Marmite, abound on Ham Nghi St around Nos 62 and 64 (**Kim Thanh**). You'll also find baby products, nappies, etc at a price.

Annam Gourmet Hai Ba Trung, 16-18 Hai Ba Trung St, T8-3822 9332, www.annam-gourmet.com. Mon-Sat 0800-2100, Sun 1000-2000. Local organic vegetables and other international delicacies at this new culinary emporium.

Circle K Vietnam, 49 Dong Du St. A mini store for basic goods.

Select Supermarket, Saigon Centre, 65 Le Loi Blvd, is a fairly decent-sized store where you can buy alcohol and all manner of processed and Western foods.

Handicrafts

Handicrafts include embroidered and woven fabrics and mother-of-pearl inlaid screens. There are dozens of shops along Dong Khoi St and Nguyen Hue Blvd.

East Meets West, 24 Le Loi Blvd. Nicely made handicrafts, reasonably priced.

Mai Handicrafts, 298 Nguyen Trong Tuyen St, Q Tan Binh, T8-3844 0988. A little way out of town but sells an interesting selection of goods, fabrics and handmade paper all made by disadvantaged people in small income-generating schemes.

Ceramics

Vietnam has a ceramics tradition going back hundreds of years. There has been a renaissance of this art in the past decade. Shops selling new and antique (or antique-looking ceramics) abound on the main shopping streets of **Dong Khoi** and **Le Thanh Ton**. There is a lot of traditional Chinese-looking blue and white and also very attractive celadon green, often with a crackled glaze. There are many other styles and finishes as local craftsmen brush the dust off old ideas and come up with new ones. **Nga Shop**, see Lacquerware, below, has a good range.

Lacquerware

Vietnamese lacquerware has a long history, and a reputation of sorts. Visitors to the workshop can witness the production process and, of course, buy the products if they wish. Lacquerware is available from many of the handicraft shops on Nguyen Hue Blvd and Dong Khoi St. Also from the **Lamson Lacquerware Factory**, 106 Nguyen Van Troi St (opposite Omni Hotel). Accepts Visa and MasterCard.

Duy Tan, 41 Ton That Thiep St, T8-382 3614. Open 1100-2000. Pretty ceramics and lacquerware.

Cong Ty 27-7, Handicapped Handicrafts, 153 Xo Viet Nghe Tinh St, T8-3840 8211, http://www.27-7.com.vn/handicraft/html/about.asp. Lacquerware and its fascinating process can be seen and bought at this outlet on the outskirts of the city. All tour operators will know where it is.

Nga Shop, 49-57 Dong Du St, T8-3823 8356, www.huongngafinearts.vn. **Nga** has become one of the best-known lacquer stores as a result of her high-quality designs. Other top-quality rosewood and ceramic handicrafts suitable for souvenirs are available.

Home furnishings and furniture

This is a new industry in Vietnam and one that has grown from nowhere to becoming very significant in global terms. Interestingly, now that Vietnam has just about cut down all its own trees, timber is imported from Borneo and Cambodia. How much comes from 'sustainable' sources no one knows – whatever they might try to tell you. One thing is certain: one heck of a lot comes from plundered forests.

Red Door Deco, 31 Le Thanh Ton St. Stylish, innovative and well-made furniture, fabrics and ornaments.

Linen

Good-quality linen table cloths and sheets are avaliable from shops on **Dong Khoi** and **Le Thanh Ton** streets.

Jewellery

Jewellery is another industry that has flourished in recent years and there is something to suit most tastes. At the cheaper end there is a cluster of gold and jewellery shops around **Ben Thanh Market** and and also in the **International Trade Centre** on Nam Ky Khoi Nghia St. In these stalls because skilled labour is so cheap one rarely pays more than the weight of the item in silver or gold. At the higher end **Therese**, with a shop in the **Caravelle Hotel**, has established an international reputation.

Outdoor gear

Vietnam produces a range of equipment for climbing and camping, such as walking boots, fleeces and rucksacks. Top-quality brand-name goods can be bought cheaply, especially from around **Pham Ngu Lao** and **De Tham** streets.

War surplus

From **Dan Sinh Market**, Yersin St, between Nguyen Thai Binh St and Nguyen Cong Tru St.

▲▲ Activities and tours

Bowling

Diamond Superbowl is on the 4th floor of **Diamond Plaza**, 34 Le Duan St, right behind the cathedral, T8-3825 7778, ext 12. 24 lanes on the top floor, which also has a fast-food outlet, video games and plenty of pool tables.

Superbowl, 43A Truong Son St, Q Tan Binh, T8-3848 8888. An enormous complex just outside the airport with 32 lanes, video arcades and fast-food outlets.

Cookery classes

Saigon Cooking Class, held at the new **Hoa Tuc** (see Eating), 74 Hai Ba Trung St, T8-3825 8485, www.saigoncookingclass.com. Children, aged 7 and above, are welcome.

Vietnam Cookery Center, 362/8 Ung Van Khiem St, Q Binh Thanh, T8-3512 2764, www.vietnamcookery.com. Offers short and in-depth courses for adults and children.

Golf

Bochang Dong Nai Golf Resort, Dong Nai Province, 50 km north of HCMC up Highway 1, T61-386 6288, http://dongnaigolf.com.vn. A very attractive 27-hole golf course with restaurant and bar and accommodation.

Golf Vietnam and Country Club, Long Thanh My Ward, Q9, T8-6280 0124, http://vietnamgolfcc.com. An internationally owned 36-hole course with an east and west course, just north of the city. The complex also has tennis and badminton courts, a boating lake and children's play-ground. On-site accommodation is available.

Song Be Golf Resort, 77 Binh Duong Blvd, Lai Thieu, Q Thuan An, Binh Duong Province, 22 km from HCMC on Highway 13, T650-375 6660, http://songbegolf.com. An attractive golf resort set in 100 ha of land with lakes and tree-lined fairways. For non-golfers there are tennis courts, a gym, sauna and children's playground.

Racing

Phu Tho Racecourse, 2 Le Dai Hanh St, Q11, T8-3962 4319, http://horseracing. vietnamracing.net. Races on Sat and Sun afternoons starting at 1200. Both the winner and the 2nd horse have to be selected to collect. The course has been reopened with financing from an interested Chinese entrepreneur and Britons plan to introduce new breeding stock to Vietnam. Beware pickpockets.

Swimming

Some hotels allow non-residents to use their pool for a fee. Decent pools are at the **Sofitel Plaza**, **Grand** and **Caravelle**.
International Club, 285B Cach Mang Thang Tam St, Q10, T8-3865 7695.
Lan Anh Club, almost next door to the **International Club** at 291 Cach Mang Thang Tam St, T8-3862 7144. Pleasant with a nice pool and tennis courts.
Saigon Water Park, Go Dua Bridge, Kha Van Can St, Q Thu Duc, T8-3897 0456, Mon-Fri 0900-1700, Sat and Sun 0900-2000. Admission is charged according to height. A little way out but is enormous fun. It has a variety of water slides of varying degrees of excitement and a child's pool on a 5-ha site. It is hugely popular with the Vietnamese.

Tennis

Tennis is possible at the **Rex Hotel** and **New World Hotel**, see Sleeping, above.
Lan Anh Club, 291 Cach Mang Thang Tam St. 20,000d per hr.

Therapies

L'Apothiquaire, 61-63 Le Thanh Ton St, T8-3822 1218, www.lapothiquaire.com. Massages, chocolate therapy, spa packages and slimming treatments in this lovely spa.
Qi Salon and Spa, Caravelle Hotel, www. qispa.com.vn. You can indulge in everything from a 20-min Indian head massage to a blow-out 5-hr Qi Special.

Vespa tours

Vietnam Vespa Adventures, Cafe Zoom, 169A De Tham St, T8-3920 3897, www. vietnamvespaadventure.com. Half-day tours of the city, 3-day tours to Mui Ne and 8-day tours to Dalat and Nha Trang. The city tours are fun, insightful and recommended. Led by Oz veteran Walter Pearson.

Tour operators

Many operators run cheap tours to and through the Mekong Delta (starting from US$10 for a day trip) and should be your 1st port of call for trips to the south as local buses will eat in to your holiday time. These trips are also useful if you want to see some of the delta but work your way into Cambodia via Chau Doc. Trips to Phu Quoc overland and back via a flight are also arranged. TNK can also book trips to the Long Tan battle memorial cross and Nui Dat battlefield for those interested in ANZAC involvement in the Second Indochina War.
Ann Tours, 58 Ton That Tung St, T8-3925 3636, www.anntours.com. Generally excellent with knowledgeable guides.
Asia Pacific Travel, 127 Ban Co St, District 3, T8-3833 4083, www.asiapacifictravel.vn. Affordable small-group adventure travel and a wide selection of tours.
Asian Trails, 5th floor, 21 Nguyen Trung Ngan St, Q1, T8-3910 2871, www.asiantrails. info. Experienced operators offering various package tours across Asia.
Buffalo Tours, Satra House, Suite 601, 58 Dong Khoi St, T8-3827 9170, www.buffalotours. com. Organizes trips to the Mekong Delta, city tours, the Cu Chi tunnels and Cao Dai Temple and arranges a home concert in HCMC with a family who have mastered and perform traditional Vietnamese instruments; this latter trip is a delightful way to spend an evening. Staff are helpful. Good countrywide operator with longstanding reputation.
Cuu Long Tourist, 190 Cong Quynh St, T8-3920 0339, cuulongtouristnet@hcm.vnn. vn, www.cuulongtourist.com. Tours and homestays from Vinh Long in the Mekong

Delta. **Cuu Long** has a monopoly on the homestays here and so you will need to book through its office here or in Vinh Long. 10-hr day trips to Vinh Long can be organized.
Delta Adventure Tours, 267 De Tham St, T8-920 2112, www.deltaadventuretours. com. Slow and express bus and boat tours through the Mekong Delta to Phnom Penh, Cambodia at very good prices.
Exotissimo, 64 Dong Du St, T8-3827 2911, www.exotissimo.com. An efficient agency that can handle all travel needs of visitors to Vietnam. Its excursions are well guided.
Fiditour, 129 Nguyen Hue Blvd, T8-3914 1516, www.fiditour.vn. Reasonably priced tour organizer with polite and helpful staff. Visa service and money exchange.
Handspan, F7, Titan Building, 18A Nam Quoc Cang St, T8-3925 7605, www. handspan.com. Wide range of tours with a commitment to sustainable tourism.
Kim Travel, 270 De Tham St, T8-3920 5552, www.kimtravel.com. Organizes minibuses to Nha Trang, Dalat, etc and tours of the Mekong; good source of information.
Saigontourist, 45 Le Thanh Ton St, T8-3829 8914, www.saigontourist.net. City and Mekong Delta tours. Longstanding operator.
SinhBalo, 283/20 Pham Ngu Lao, T8-3837 6765, www.sinhbalo.com. Mr Sinh, formerly of Sinh Café, is a recommended tour operator organizing tours including cycling, adventure and cross-country tours.
Sinh Tourist (formerly Sinh Café), 246-248 De Tham St, T8-3838 9597, www. thesinhtourist.vn. **Sinh Tourist** now has branches and agents in all main towns in Vietnam. Its tours are generally good value and its open ticket is excellent value. For many people, especially budget travellers, **Sinh** is the first port of call. It is tempting to tour the entire country with them as it makes travelling easy. Like many other tour operators, trips to the Mekong Delta (from180,000d) and onwards to Cambodia are organized (from 580,000d). It also offers round trip bus and plane journeys to Phnom Penh and Siem Reap. The company also

deals with visa extensions, flight, train and hotel bookings and car rentals. Children under 2 are free; 2- to 5-year-olds are charged 75% of the full price. Beware that there are numerous copycat **Sinh Cafés**; make sure you know which ones are the real deal as many of the fake Sinhs are to be avoided. This one is the HQ.
TM Brother's Café, 230 De Tham St, T8-3837 7764, tmbrothertours@yahoo.com. The genuine version is a reliable Open Tour Bus operator. It also runs trips around the Mekong Delta, bus services to Delta towns, and trips on to Cambodia; also to Phu Quoc by land and ferry (US$29).
TNK Travel, 222 De Tham St, 40 Bui Vien St and 161 Pham Ngu Lao St, T8-3920 4766, www.tnktravel.com.vn. Open Tour Bus trips as well as trips to the Mekong Delta and on to Cambodia. Very helpful.
Vidotour, 145 Nam Ky Khoi Nghia St, Q3, T8-3933 0457, www.vidotourtravel.com. One of the most efficient organizers of group travel in the country. Its website contains useful travel news on Indochina.

⊖ Transport

HCMC will get a much-needed mass rapid transit system in the next 5 years with 22 stations in the downtown area and there are plans to eventually move the international airport to a site east of HCMC.

Air
Airport information
Tan Son Nhat Airport, 49 Troung Son, Tan Binh, T8-3844 8358, www.saigonairport.com, is 30 mins northwest of the city, depending on the traffic. The new international terminal opened in 2007; the old terminal building is now the domestic terminal.

Airport facilities include banks and ATMs and 2 locker rooms from US$1 a bag for 10 hrs (T8-3848 5383, 0700-2230 daily), a Vietnam Airlines desk, a post office, information desk. **Lost and found** T8-3844 6665 ext 7461.

Official taxis from the Saigon Airport Corporation (T8-3866 6666) to the city centre cost 140,000d. By doing it this way you avoid the hordes of taxi drivers who will swamp you as you exit.

Bus No 152 runs from the airport to town every 50 mins, 30 mins, 6000d one way. The bus goes to Pham Ngu Lao backpacker area and then to Benh Thanh Market and on to Dong Khoi St.

HCMC is connected to every airport in the country except Dien Bien Phu..

Flights to **Con Dao** are 3 times daily, 55 mins.

Airline offices

AirAsia, 254 De Tham St, T8-3838 9810, www.airasia.com. **Air France**, 130 Dong Khoi St, T8-3829 0981, www.airfrance.com. **Bangkok Airways**, Unit 103, Saigon Trade Center, 37 Ton Duc Thang St, T8-3910 4490, www.bangkokair.com. **Cathay Pacific**, 72-74 Nguyen Thi Minh Khai St, T8-3822 3203, www.cathaypacific.com. **Emirate Airlines**, 170-172 Nam Ky Khoi Nghia, Q3, T8-3930 2939, www.emirates.com. **Eva Air**, 2A-4A, Ton Duc Thang St, T8-3844 5211, www.evaair.com. **Gulf Air**, 18 Dang Thi Nhu St, Q1, T8-3915 7614, www.gulfair.com. **JAL**, www.jal.co.jp. **Jetstar**, 112 Hong Ha, Q Tan Binh, T8-3845 0092, www.jetstar.com. **Lao Airlines**, www.laoairlines.com. **Lufthansa**, 19-25 Nguyen Hue Blvd, T8-3829 8529, www.lufthansa.com. **Malaysia**, Saigon Trade Center, 37 Ton Duc Thang St, T8-3829 2529, www.malaysiaairlines.com. **Qantas**, HT&T Vietnam, Level 2, Ben Thanh TSC Building, 186-188 Le Thanh Ton St, T8-3910 5373, www.quantas.com.au. **Qatar**, Suite 8, Petro Vietnam Tower, 1-5 Le Duan St, T8-3827 3777, www.qatarairways.com. **Singapore Airlines**, 29 Le Duan St, T8-3823 1588, www.singaporeair.com. **Thai Airways**, 29 Le Duan St, T8-3822 3365, www.thaiairways.com.vn. **Tiger Airways**, T1206 0114, www.tigerairways.com. **Vietnam Airlines**, 6th floor, Sun Wah Tower, 115 Nguyen Hue St, T8-3832 0320, www.vietnamairlines.com. Mon-Fri 0800-1830, Sat 0800-1200, 1330-1700.

Bicycle and motorbike

If staying in HCMC for any length of time it might be a good idea to buy a bicycle (see Shopping, above, and page 24). Alternatively, bikes can be hired for around US$3 a day in Pham Ngu Lao.

Motorbikes can be hired from some of the cheaper hotels and travel cafés, especially in Pham Ngu Lao St for around US$5-10 per day depending on the age, manual or automatic model, and model of the bike. Bikes should always be parked in the roped-off compounds (*Gui xe*) that are all over town; they will be looked after for a small charge (12,000d – always get a ticket).

Bus
Local

The bus service in HCMC has now become more reliable and frequent: it is really quite a useful means of getting about. The buses are green or yellow and are a safer and cheaper (even in some cases more convenient) alternative to any other modes of transport in HCMC. They run at intervals of 10-20 mins – depending on the time of day. In rush hours they are jammed with passengers and can run late. There are bus stops every 500 m. The same price – 3000d per person – applies to all routes.

All these buses start from or stop by the Ben Thanh bus station opposite Ben Thanh Market, T8-3821 4444. A free map of all bus routes can also be obtained here in the chaotic waiting room. Buses depart here for Vung Tau and Cu Chi.

No 1 Saigon – China Town (Cho Binh Tay). From the bus stop, you can walk to Cho Lon Bus Station (Ben Xe Cho Lon), 86 Trang Tu, Q5, T8-3855 7719, where there are buses to **Tien Giang**, **Long An** and **Ben Tre**), 0500-2130.

No 2 Saigon – Western Coach Station (Ben Xe Mien Tay), 137 Hung Vuong, Q Binh Chanh, T8-3877 6593. Buses to the south and **Mekong Delta**, 0445-1900.

No 26 Ben Thanh Market – Eastern Coach Station (Ben Xe Mien Dong), 227/6 Highway 13, Q Binh Thanh, T8-3877 6593. Buses to provinces in the north and **Vung Tau**, 0500-1930.

No 28 Ben Thanh Market – Tan Son Nhat (a bit misleading – it stops beside Super Bowl, 700 m from the airport), 0530-1840.

No 152 Ben Thanh Market – Tan Son Nhat Airport (straight to the airport – very often empty), 0615-1900.

Long distance

With the completion of a new ring road around HCMC, long-distance public buses, unless specifically signed Saigon or 'Ben Xe Ben Thanh' do not come into the city. Passengers are dropped off on the ring road at Binh Phuoc bridge. From here it is a 45-min *xe ôm* journey into town. Therefore always try to catch a bus heading into the town centre, such as one of the Open Tour Buses. A fleet of a/c buses connects central HCMC with the bus terminals, 3000d. These connecting buses depart from the bus station opposite Ben Thanh Market.

From **Mien Dong Terminal**, north of the city, buses north to **Dalat**, **Hué**, **Danang** and all significant points on the road to Hanoi. The **Hoang Long** bus company runs 11 deluxe buses daily to **Hanoi**, T8-2243 8990, with comfortable beds, 690,000d one way, including all meals and drinks, 36 hrs. Also an office at 47 Pham Ngu Lao, T8-915 1818, https://hoanglongasia.com.

From **Mien Tay Terminal**, some distance southwest of town, buses south to the **Mekong Delta** towns.There is also a bus station in **Cholon** which serves destinations such as **Long An**, **My Thuan**, **Ben Luc** and **My Tho**.

Minibus

Minibuses for **Vung Tau** depart from Ham Nghi St – hop in quickly as they are not meant to pick up passengers in town. **Mai Linh Express**, 201 Pham Ngu Lao, T8-3920 2929, www.mailinh.vn, runs minivans or small coaches to the Mekong Delta and other southern Vietnam destinations.

Open Tour Bus

Numerous Open Tour Buses start their journey from HCMC with first stops being either **Dalat**, **Mui Ne** or **Nha Trang**. See under tour operators, page 59.

International bus

Many tour operators run tours and transport to Cambodia (see Tour operators, page 342) crossing the border at **Moc Bai**. Visas for Cambodia can be bought at the border for around US$25. **Mai Linh**, T8-3920 2929, runs to **Phnom Penh**, 0630, 0830, 1300, 1430, US$11, 6 hrs from 201 Pham Ngu Lao. **Sapaco Tourist**, 309-327 Pham Ngu Lao St, T8-3920 3623, www.sapacotourist.com, runs buses from Pham Ngu Lao to **Phnom Penh** from 0600-1400, 8 daily, US$12, 6 hrs; at 0600 to **Siem Reap**, US$20, 12 hrs. Buses return at 0700 from Siem Reap and between 0600-1500 from Phnom Penh to HCMC. **TNK** runs daily buses (0800-1400) hourly to **Phnom Penh**, US$12. Or take a tour with a company like **Sinh** that will ensure you see a bit of the Mekong Delta before ending up in Phnom Penh.

Cyclos

Cyclos are a peaceful way to get around the city. They can be hired by the hour (approximately 250,000d per hr) or to reach a specific destination. Some drivers speak English. Each tends to have his own patch which is jealously guarded. Expect to pay more outside the major hotels – it is worth walking around the corner.

Cyclos are much rarer now but can be found waiting in tourist spots. Some visitors complain of cyclo drivers in HCMC 'forgetting' the agreed price (though Hanoi is worse). Cyclos are being banned from more and more streets in the centre of HCMC, which may involve a longer and more expensive journey. This is the excuse trotted out

On the move

Traffic in Ho Chi Minh City is out of control. In fact, traffic in Vietnam is madder than it has ever been, but at last officials have decided to act.

By 2013 the economic power-house is to get six metro stations to shuffle commuters in and out from the suburbs. This is not a year too late. Ho Chi Minh City throbs with eight million people, four million motorbikes and more than 400,000 cars contributing to a polluted pool and traffic gridlock in rush hour. An additional one million motorbikes and 60,000 cars commute in on a daily basis. (In comparison, London is home to 7.5 million people and 2.5 million cars.)

Restrictions on buying a motorbike were lifted in 2006 after a three-year ban to try to reduce the number of bikes on the road and although the city introduced more buses – some 3300 in the same three-year period – more than 750,000 new motos swerved onto the roads.

There are 20,000 accidents every year and 40 deaths a day according to the Ministry of Transport (see also box, page 24).

But it's the train that is the future in Vietnam. Heavy investment is to be made in railways, partly to reduce traffic on the roads, officials say. Not only are the Japanese involved in a brand new north-south railway but they are in talks with city officials to build an urban railway system using mass rapid transit trains. Six US$6bn subway routes covering 107 km are under construction: The first underground section will run 2.6 km from Ben Thanh Market to Ba Son Shipyard. Three tramlines including one from Cholon to Mien Tay bus station will be built.

A new express north-south railway project costing US$32.6 billion has been cancelled. The government said it would not serve the majority of the population and local people could not afford the fares.

---

every time (particularly if extra money is demanded) and it is invariably true. If taking a tour agree a time and price and point to watches and agree on the start time. One scam involves drivers arguing you have used up more than the agreed time and shouting in the street that you are pulling a fast one. Do not be humiliated into offering more than the agreed price because of the shouting.

Hydrofoil
There are 2 or 3 'competing' companies which operate hydrofoils from the wharf at the end of Ham Nghi St in HCMC to Halong St jetty in Vung Tau.

Greenlines, office on the jetty and at 51 Ham Nghi, T8-3821 5609, www.taucanhngam.com, 180,000d; children 90,000d. Same deal as **Petro Express**.

Petro Express, on the jetty. First service 0630 and then 4 services until 1645-1700.

Vina Express, www.vinaexpress.com.vn. 13 services a day from 0630-1645.

Taxi
HCMC has quite a large fleet of meter taxis. There are more than 14 taxi companies fighting bitterly for trade. Competition has brought down prices so they are now reasonably inexpensive and for 2 or more are cheaper than cyclos or xe ôm.

All taxis are metered, ensure it is set after you get in. Prices start at between 12,000d-15,000d for the first 1.5-2 km reducing after that to, for example, 8500d with **Vinasun**, cheaper than say, **Saigon Tourist**. The standard of vehicle and service vary widely. All taxis are numbered; in the event of forgotten luggage or other problems ring the company and quote the number of your taxi.

Taxi tips Taxi scams, especially in HCMC and Hanoi, are rife beyond belief. If the meter is 'not working' (which is illegal) get out and get another cab, otherwise you will be ripped off. If the meter starts doubling and tripling, ask to stop and get out and pay the fare or, if you know the city and the fare for your trip, get out and pay the fare you think it should have been. If you can, avoid taxis hovering outside late-night establishments. Walk away from the place and hail a cab on the road or walk to a hotel with a taxi rank. If you think you have been overcharged and you are arriving at a hotel or restaurant, get out and ask the establishment staff to help.

Take only taxis listed below (Vinataxi, Mai Linh and Vinasun are the best):

Mai Linh Taxi (green and white, note that the Deluxe version is more expensive), T8-3822 2666, www.mailinh.vn. Saigontourist, T8-3845 0912. Vinasun (white), T8-3827 2727. Vinataxi (yellow), T8-3811 1111.

Motorcycle taxis
Honda or *xe ôm* are the quickest way to get around town and cheaper than cyclos; agree a price and hop on the back. *Xe ôm* drivers can be recognized by their baseball caps, and tendency to chain smoke; they hang around on most street corners. Short journeys should be around 10-15,000d but you may end up paying more.

Train
The station (*Nha ga*) is 2 km from the centre of the city at 1 Nguyen Thong St, Q3, T8-3931 2795. Facilities for the traveller are much improved and include a/c waiting room, post office and bank (no TCs). Regular daily connections with **Hanoi** and all points north. Trains take between 29½ and 42½ hrs to reach Hanoi; hard and soft berths are available. Sleepers should be booked in advance. (See Essentials, page 38, for more information on rail travel.)

There is now a **Train Booking Agency** at 275c Pham Ngu Lao St, T8-3836 7640, 0730-1830, which saves an unnecessary journey out to the station. Alternatively, for a small

fee, most travel agents will obtain tickets. The railway timetable can be seen online at www.vr.com.vn.

Directory

Banks
There are now dozens of ATMs in shops, hotels and banks. Remember to take your passport if cashing TCs and withdrawing money from a card.

ANZ Bank, 2 Ngo Duc Ke St, T8-3829 9319, www.anz.com/vietnam. 2% commission charged on cashing TCs into US dollars or dong, ATM. **HSBC, Hong Kong** and **Shanghai Bank**, 235 Dong Khoi St, T8-3829 2288. Provides all financial services, 2% commission on TCs, ATM. **Sacombank**, 11-213 Pham Ngu Lao St, Q1, T8-3837 1526.

Embassies and consulates
Australia, Landmark Building, 5B Ton Duc Thang St, T8-3521 8100, www.hcmc.vietnam. embassy.gov.au. **Cambodia**, 41 Phung Khac Khoan St, T8-3829 2751. **Canada**, 235 Dong Khoi St, T8-3827 9899, www. canadainternational.gc.ca. **China**, 39 Nguyen Thi Minh Khai St, T8-3829 2457. **France**, 27 Nguyen Thi Minh Khai St, T8-3520 6800, www.consulfrance-hcm.org. **Germany**, 126 Nguyen Dinh Chieu St, Q3, T8-3829 2455. **Italy**, 91 Nguyen Huu Canh St, Binh Thanh District, T8-3514 4937, www.ambhanoi.esteri. it. **Japan**, 13-17 Nguyen Hue Blvd, T8-3822 5314. **Laos**, 9B Pasteur St, T8-3829 7667. **Malaysia**, 2 Ngo Duc Ke St, T8-3829 9023. **Netherlands**, Saigon Tower, 29 Le Duan St, T8-3823 5932, http://www.mfa.nl/hcm-en. **New Zealand**, Suite 909, Metropole Building, 235 Dong Khoi St, T8-3822 6907. **Singapore**, 65 Le Loi Blvd, T8-3822 5174, www.mfa.gov. sg/hochiminhcity/. **Sweden**, 8A/11D1 Thai Van Lung St, T8-3823 6800. **Switzerland**, 42 Giang Minh St, T8-3744 6996. **Thailand**, 77 Tran Quoc Thao St, Q3, T8-3932 7637. **UK**, 25 Le Duan St, T8-3829 8433. **USA**, 4 Le Duan St, T8-3520 4200, http://hochiminh.usconsulate.gov.

Hospitals

Cho Ray Hospital, 201B Nguyen Chi Thanh Blvd, Q5, T8-3855 3137, www.choray.org. vn. **Colombia-Gia Dinh International Clinic**, 1 No Trang Long St, Q Binh Thanh, T8-3803 1104. American-run emergency clinic with medivac and General Practice services. **Colombia Asia** (Saigon International Clinic), 8 Alexander de Rhodes St, T8-3823 8455, www.columbiaasia.com. International doctors. **French Vietnam Hospital**, 6 Nguyen Luong Bang St, Saigon South, Q7, T8-5411 3333, www.fvhospital.com. **Family Medical Practice Ho Chi Minh City**, Diamond Plaza, 34 Le Duan St, T8-3822 7848, www.vietnammedicalpractice.com. Well-equipped practice, 24-hr emergency service and an evacuation service; Australian and European doctors. Also provides a useful major and minor disease outbreak service on its website. **International SOS**, 167 Nam Ky Khoi Nghia St, Q3, T8-3829 8424, www.internationalsos.com. Comprehensive 24-hr medical and dental service and medical evacuating.

Immigration office

Immigration office, 254 Nguyen Trai St, T8-3832 2300. Changes visa to specify overland exit via Moc Bai if travelling to Cambodia, or for overland travel to Laos or China. Also for visa extensions but a tour operator offering this service could save you time and hassle.

Internet

There are a number of internet cafés in the Pham Ngu Lao area. Virtually all hotels and guesthouses in the city offer email services and Wi-Fi.

Laundry

There are several places that will do your laundry around Pham Ngu Lao St.

Police

Police,161 Nguyen Du St. The police will not resolve anything but if you are the victim of a robbery or crime you will need a crime report for an insurance claim. Do not even think about attending a police station without a translator.

Post office and telephone

GPO, 2 Cong Xa Paris (facing the cathedral), 0630-2100. Telex, telegram and international telephone services available. **Vinaphone** and **Mobiphone**, the local mobile phone providers, both have offices around the general PO building for the sale of pre-pay sim cards. Much cheaper than using an overseas sim card in Vietnam. You can also buy **mobicards** from **Shop & Go JSC**, 74A Hai Ba Trung St, near the Park Hyatt and from other outlets displaying the stickers.

Contents

Footprint features

Mekong Delta

Ins and outs

Getting there

Follow Highway 1 from Ho Chi Minh City and it will take you as far as Can Tho passing through Vinh Long and My Tho along the way. There are several highways throughout the region linking the major towns. Highway 1 from Ho Chi Minh City goes to My Tho, Vinh Long and ends in Can Tho. Highways 80 and 50 are reasonably good and Highway 91 is improving. The road is relatively good from Ho Chi Minh City to Can Tho, Long Xuyen and Chau Doc, but beyond these towns roads are narrow and pot-holed and travel is generally slow, although it is improving. Roads, however, are dangerous, especially for motorbike drivers – so much so that the large number of placards that used to dot the Mekong warning against the dangers of HIV have, in the main, been replaced with billboards warning of the dangers of driving too fast.

Ferry crossings slow travel down still further and if travelling by bus expect long waits in queues (private cars push straight to the front). The huge My Thuan suspension bridge, a major Australian aid project just outside Vinh Long, has eliminated one ferry trip and made the journey quicker and smoother. Other new bridges have opened – My Tho and Ben Tre, once an island province and backwater, are now linked. In Chau Doc a new bridge links the city to Con Tien village and thus connects to a road to the Cambodian border at Khanh Binh but this is not yet an international border crossing. A 2.7-km bridge over the Hau River linking up Highway 1 in Vinh Long Province to Can Tho city opened in April 2010. Some ferries do still cross to and from Can Tho from the ferry piers. Public long-distance boat services have ceased from Can Tho. The **Victoria** hotel chain operates a boat service for its guests between Chau Doc and Phnom Penh.

It is possible to fly from Ho Chi Minh City to Phu Quoc Island and Rach Gia daily and sometimes to Ca Mau. Currently there are flights from Hanoi to Can Tho.

Ho Chi Minh City tour operators run tours to Can Tho, My Tho and Chau Doc and agents within these towns run tours to surrounding sights and organize onward transport. Many local and Ho Chi Minh City operators also arrange boat and bus transport to Phnom Penh, Cambodia. ▸▸ *See also Tour operators, pages 82, 93, 108 and 115 and Transport, pages 82, 94 and 108.*

Getting around

There are the ubiquitous *Honda ôms* and also, in the major towns, taxis, *xe lôi* and public bus services are plentiful and efficient. Also there are many river taxis available and – not used anywhere else in Vietnam – the sampan.

Best time to visit

The months December to May are when the Mekong Delta is at its best. During the monsoon from June to November the weather is poor with constant background drizzle interrupted by bursts of torrential rain. In October flooding may interrupt movement particularly in the remoter areas and around Chau Doc and Dong Thap Province.

Background

The region has had a restless history. Conflict between Cambodians and Vietnamese for ownership of the wide plains resulted in ultimate Viet supremacy although important Khmer relics remain. But it was during the French and American wars that the Mekong Delta produced many of the most fervent fighters for independence.

The Mekong Delta or Cuu Long (Nine Dragons) is Vietnam's rice bowl and, before the partition of the country in 1954, rice was traded from the south where there was a rice surplus, to the north where there was a rice deficit, as well as internationally. Even prior to the creation of French Cochin China in the 19th century, rice was being transported from here to Hué, the imperial capital. The delta covers 67,000 sq km, of which about half is cultivated. Rice yields are in fact generally lower than in the north, but the huge area under cultivation and the larger size of farms means that both individual households and the region produce a surplus for export. In the Mekong Delta there is nearly three times as much rice land per person as there is in the north. It is this that accounts for the relative wealth of the region.

The Mekong Delta was not opened up to agriculture on an extensive scale until the late 19th and early 20th centuries. Initially it seems that this was a spontaneous process: peasants, responding to the market incentives introduced by the French, slowly began to push the frontier of cultivation southwards into this wilderness area. The process gathered pace when the French colonial government began to construct canals and drainage projects to open more land to wet rice agriculture. By the 1930s the population of the delta had reached 4.5 million with 2,200,000 ha of land under rice cultivation. The Mekong Delta, along with the Irrawaddy (Burma) and Chao Phraya (Thailand) became one of the great rice exporting areas of Southeast Asia, shipping over 1.2 million tonnes annually.

Given their proximity to prosperous Ho Chi Minh City the inhabitants of the Mekong Delta might have expected some of the benefits of development to trickle their way: in this they have largely been disappointed. Most of the Mekong Delta provinces are trying and to a degree securing investment into their respective provinces. Be it hotels, cafés, karaoke in Ha Tien to canning and storage plants in Can Tho, they are trying to improve their collective lot. The main problem that they face is that everyone knows that each year during the monsoon season wide areas of the Mekong flood. The government is slowly but surely building up river defences against the annual floods but it is a laborious process. Tourist services are improving year on year.

My Tho and around

My Tho is an important riverside market town, 5 km off the main highway to Vinh Long, and is the capital of Tien Giang Province. It is the stepping-off point for boat trips to islands in the Tien River. Visitors enjoy the chance to wander among abundant fruit orchards and witness at first hand local industries. My Tho is 71 km southwest of Ho Chi Minh City on the banks of the Tien River, a distributary of the Mekong. The drive from Ho Chi Minh City is dispiriting, nose-to-tail traffic and virtually uninterrupted ribbon development testify to the population pressure in so much of this land. The town has had a turbulent history: it was Khmer until the 17th century, when the advancing Vietnamese took control of the surrounding area. In the 18th century Thai forces annexed the territory, before being driven out in 1784. Finally, the French gained control in 1862. Around My Tho are the northern delta towns of Ben Tre, Vinh Long, Tra Vinh, Sa Dec and Cao Lanh.

▶ *For listings, see pages 78-84.*

Ins and outs

Getting there and around The much-improved Highway 1 is the main route from Ho Chi Minh City to My Tho. There is an efficient public bus service, taxis aplenty, a few river taxis and boats and *Honda ôm*. ▶ *See Transport, page 82.*

Tourist information Tien Giang Tourist ① *8 30 Thang 4 St on the river, Ward 1, T730-387 3184, www.tiengiangtourist.com*. It has improved its services and attitude a good deal. Competition has opened up in the area but it has a near monopoly on the popular boat trips. The staff are friendly and helpful and have a good command of several languages.

My Tho → *For listings, see pages 78-84.*

On the corner of Nguyen Trai Street and Hung Vuong Street, and five minutes' walk from the central market, is **My Tho church** painted with a yellow wash with a newer, white campanile. The **central market** covers a large area from Le Loi Street down to the river. The river is the most enjoyable spot to watch My Tho life go by.

It is a long walk to **Vinh Trang Pagoda** ① *60 Nguyen Trung Trac St, daily 0900-1200, 1400-1700 (best to go by bicycle or Honda ôm)*. The entrance to the temple is through an ornate porcelain-encrusted gate. The pagoda was built in 1849 and displays a mixture of architectural styles: Chinese, Vietnamese and colonial. The façade is almost fairytale in inspiration. Two huge new statues of the Buddha now dominate the area.

There has been a flurry of municipal activity in the past couple of years not much of it beneficial. All the bustling cafés along Trung Trac Street by the side of the small Bao Dinh River have been swept away and in their place is a broad, scorched pavement devoid of any shade. The saving grace, however is the new corner café from where you can idly pass the time watching the river and passing motorbikes.

Around My Tho

The islands
There are four islands in the Tien River between My Tho and Ben Tre: Dragon, Tortoise, Phoenix and Unicorn. The best way of getting to them is to take a tour. A vast pier and boat service centre has been built on 30 Thang 4 Street where all the tour operators are now concentrated. To avoid the hundreds of visitors now descending on these islands, go in the afternoon after the tour buses have gone. Hiring a private boat (US$10) is not

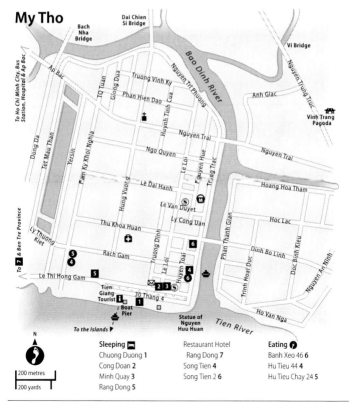

My Tho

Sleeping 🛏	Restaurant Hotel	Eating 🍴
Chuong Duong 1	Rang Dong 7	Banh Xeo 46 6
Cong Doan 2	Song Tien 4	Hu Tieu 44 4
Minh Quay 3	Song Tien 2 6	Hu Tieu Chay 24 5
Rang Dong 5		

recommended due to the lack of insurance, the communication difficulties and lack of explanations. Prices vary according to the number of people and which islands you choose to visit. ►► See Tour operators, page 82.

Immediately opposite My Tho is Dragon Island, **Tan Long Island**. It is pleasant to wander along its narrow paths. Tan Long is noted for its longan production but there are many other fruits to sample as well as honey and rice whisky.

The Island of the Coconut Monk, also known as **Con Phung (Phoenix Island)**, is about 3 km from My Tho. The 'Coconut Monk' established a retreat on this island shortly after the end of the Second World War where he developed a new 'religion', a fusion of Buddhism and Christianity. He is said to have meditated for three years on a stone slab, eating nothing but coconuts – hence the name. Persecuted by both the South Vietnamese government and by the communists, the monastery has fallen into disuse.

Unicorn Island is a garden of Eden – stuffed with longan, durian, roses, pomelo and a host of other fruit trees. Honey is made on this island too.

Ap Bac

Not far from My Tho is the hamlet of Ap Bac, the site of the communists' first major military victory against the ARVN. The battle demonstrated that without direct US involvement the communists could never be defeated. John Paul Vann was harsh in his criticism of the tactics and motivation of the South Vietnamese Army who failed to dislodge a weak VC position. As he observed from the air, almost speechless with rage, he realized how feeble his Vietnamese ally was; an opinion that few senior US officers heeded – to their cost (see *Bright Shining Lie* by Neil Sheehan).

Ben Tre → *For listings, see pages 78-84.*

Ben Tre is a typical Vietnamese delta town with a charming riverfront feel. The small bridge over the river is wooden slatted but with iron supports. Bountiful fruit stalls are laid out on the waterfront and locals sell potted plants on barges by the river. Small cargo ships pass dilapidated shacks falling into the muddy waters. Ben Tre used to be a bit of a cul-de-sac but this is changing due to the opening of the new bridge linking it to My Tho. Consequently, it doesn't attract a lot of foreign or, for that matter, Vietnamese visitors. Its main claim to fame is that it is the birthplace of Nguyen Dinh Chieu, a blind and patriotic poet. The province is essentially a huge island of mud at one of the nine mouths of the Mekong. It depends heavily on farming, fishing and coconuts although there are some light industries engaged in processing the local farm output and refining sugar. During the wars of resistance against the French and Americans, Ben Tre earned itself a reputation as a staunch Viet Minh/Viet Cong stronghold. Ben Tre in recent years has improved its tourism facilities.

Ins and outs

Getting there and around Ben Tre is no longer an island province; a bridge links it from just outside My Tho. In the city itself there are taxis and *Honda ôms*. There are also river taxis.

Tourist information Ben Tre Tourist ① *16 Hai Ba Trung St, T75-382 2392, www.bentre tourist.vn*, is friendly and helpful. The tours that it offers are not particularly cheap but it does provide a reasonable selection.

Hydrology of the Mekong Delta

The Mekong River enters Vietnam in two branches known traditionally as the Mekong and the Bassac but now called the Tien and the Hau. Over the 200-km journey to the sea they divide to form nine mouths, the so-called Nine Dragons or *Cuu Long*.

In response to the rains of the Southwest monsoon, river levels begin to rise in June, usually reaching a peak in October and falling to normal in December. This seasonal pattern is ideal for rice growing, around which the whole way of life of the delta has evolved.

The Mekong has a unique natural flood regulator in the form of Cambodia's great lake, the Tonlé Sap. As river levels rise the water backs up into the vast lake which more than doubles in size, preventing more serious flooding in the Mekong Delta. Nevertheless, the Tien and Hau still burst their banks and water inundates the huge Plain of Reeds (*Dong Thap Muoi*) and the Rach Gia Depression, home to thousands of water birds.

The annual flood has always been regarded as a blessing bringing, as it does, fertile silt and flushing out salinity and acidity from the soil. Since the 1990s, however, frequent serious flooding has made this annual event less benign and an increasingly serious problem.

From 1705 onwards Vietnamese emperors began building canals to improve navigation in the delta. This task was taken up enthusiastically by the French in order to open up new areas of the delta to rice cultivation and export. Interestingly it is thought the canals built prior to 1975 had little effect on flooding.

Since 1975 a number of new canals have been built in Cambodia and Vietnam and old ones deepened. The purpose of some of these predominantly west–east canals is to carry irrigation water to drier parts. Their effect has been to speed up the flow of water across the delta from about 17 days to five. Peak flows across the border from Cambodia have tripled in 30 years, partly as a result of deforestation and urbanization upriver.

In addition, the road network of the delta has been developed and roads raised above the normal high-water levels. This has the effect of trapping floodwater, preventing it from reaching the Gulf of Thailand or East Sea and prolonging floods. Many canals have gates to prevent the inundation of sea water; the gates also hinder the outflow of floodwaters.

Information taken from a paper by Quang M Nguyen

Sights

Vien Minh Pagoda is located on Nguyen Dinh Chieu Street and is the centre for the association of Buddhists in Ben Tre Province. It was originally made of wood but was rebuilt using concrete in 1958.

At **Binh Phu** village, 2 km from downtown, you can see rice wine being made. **Phu Le** village also makes rice wine.

Nguyen Dinh Chieu Temple is 36 km from the town centre in An Duc village. The temple is dedicated to the poet Nguyen Dinh Chieu who is Ben Tre's most famous son. It is well kept and photogenic and worth a visit. The monks are friendly and helpful.

Vinh Long is a rather ramshackle, but nonetheless clean, riverside town on the banks of the Co Chien River and is the capital of Vinh Long Province. It is the launch pad for lovely boat trips through An Binh Island via the small floating market at Cai Be. An Binh is the centre of the Mekong homestay industry (see box, page 79).

At sunset families cluster along the river promenade to fly colourful kites in animal shapes. In the mornings, puppies and watermelons are for sale along Hung Dao Vuong Street and teenagers play ball and throw home-made shuttlecocks in the afternoons along Hung Vuong Street.

Vinh Long was one of the focal points in the spread of Christianity in the Mekong Delta and there is a cathedral and Roman Catholic seminary in town. The richly stocked and well-ordered Cho Vinh Long (central market), is on 1 Thang 5 Street down from the **Cuu Long** hotel and stretches back to near the local bus station. A new market building has also been built opposite the existing market. There is a Cao Dai church not far from the second bridge leading into town from Ho Chi Minh City and My Tho, visible on the right-hand side. In the countryside around Vinh Long you will see dozens of egg-shaped brick mounds – these are terracotta-coloured kilns for the brick works and are an attractive sight. Vinh Long makes a reasonable stopping-off point on the road to Long Xuyen, Rach Gia and Ha Tien.

Ins and outs

Getting there and around The road runs direct from Ho Chi Minh City via the My Thuan bridge. There are good connections to all other Mekong towns. There is a good bus service and *Honda ôms*. ▸▸ *See Transport, page 82.*

Tourist information Cuu Long Tourist ① *No 1, 1 Thang 5 St, T70-382 3616, http:// cuulongtourist.com, daily 0700-1700.* Ask for Mr Phu, he is helpful, and has a good understanding of English and French. This is one of the friendlier and more helpful of the state-run companies and runs tours and homestays. ▸▸ *See Tour operators, page 366.*

Sights

The **river trips** taking in the islands and orchards around Vinh Long are as charming as any in the delta, but getting there can be expensive. See tour operators, page 82. Local boatmen are prepared to risk a fine and take tourists for one-tenth of the operators' charge. **Binh Hoa Phuoc Island** and An Binh, generally collectively known as An Binh, make a pleasant side trip, see also Sleeping. There is a **floating market** at Cai Be, about 10 km from Vinh Long. This is not quite so spectacular as the floating markets around Can Tho (see page 87) but nevertheless make for a diverting morning's trip.

An Binh Island, just a 10-minute ferry ride from Phan Boi Chau Street, represents a great example of delta landscape. The island can be explored either by boat, paddling down narrow canals, or by following the dirt tracks and crossing monkey bridges on foot. Monkey bridges are those single bamboo poles with, if you are lucky, a flimsy handrail which is there for psychological reassurance rather than to stop you from falling off. But don't worry, the water is warm and usually shallow and the mud soft. On the island is the ancient **Tien Chau Pagoda** and a *nuoc mam* (**fish sauce factory**).

The **Vinh Long Museum** ① *T70-382 3181, daily 0800-1100 and 1330-1630, Fri-Sun 1800-2100, free,* displays photographs of the war including the devastation of the town in 1968, some weaponry and a room dedicated to Ho Chi Minh.

The **Van Thieu Mieu Temple** ① *0500-1100, 1300-1900*, a charming mustard yellow cluster of buildings is 2 km from town along Tran Phu Street. In the first building to the right on entering the complex is an altar dedicated to Confucius.

The Khmer Temples at Tra Vinh (see below) can be visited on a day trip from Vinh Long.

Tra Vinh → *For listings, see pages 78-84.*

Tra Vinh is the capital of the province of the same name and has a large Khmer population – 300,000 people (30% of the province's population) are Khmer, and at the last count there were 140 Khmer temples. The large Khmer population is a bit of an enigma, for while Khmer people can be found across the Mekong Delta the concentration is highest in this, the most distant Mekong province from Cambodia. For whatever reason, Tra Vinh established itself as a centre of population some 500 years ago; then, as Vietnamese settlers began fanning across the delta displacing the Khmer, the population of this area remained firmly rooted creating a little pocket of Cambodian ethnicity and culture far from home. The modern market building, adorned with a huge picture of Ho Chi Minh, is the pivot of the city.

Ins and outs
Getting there and around The road is direct from Vinh Long and then follow the signs. There are quite a few taxis, plenty of *Honda ôm* and a reasonable domestic bus service. As the majority of town is shaded thanks to the tree-lined boulevards most people walk.

Tourist information **Tra Vinh Tourist** ① *64-66 Le Loi St, T74-385 8556, travinhtourist@yahoo. com*, owns the **Cuu Long Hotel** and is friendly and helpful. City tour by moto from US$18.

Background
For those interested in religious edifices Tra Vinh is the place to visit. In one of the more obscure surveys undertaken to calculate the number of religious buildings per head of population it was found that with more than 140 Khmer temples, 50 Vietnamese pagodas, five Chinese pagodas, seven mosques and 14 churches serving a town of only 70,000 souls Tra Vinh was the outright winner by miles.

So many attractive buildings coupled with the tree-lined boulevards – some trees are well over 30-m tall – make this one of the more attractive cities in the Delta. It is well worth an overnight stay here to recharge the batteries.

Sights
The **market** is on the central square between Dien Bien Phu Street – the town's main thoroughfare – and the Tra Vinh River, which is a relatively small branch of the Mekong compared with most Delta towns. A walk through the market and along the river bank makes a pleasant late afternoon or early evening stroll. Otherwise there is not a lot to do in Tra Vinh, although it's a nice enough place to spend some time. The **Ong Met Pagoda** on Dien Bien Phu Street north of the town centre dates back to the mid-16th century. It is a gilded Chinese-style temple where the monks will be only too happy to ply you with tea and practice their English, although the building itself is fairly unremarkable.

Around Tra Vinh
The two best reasons to come to Tra Vinh are to see the storks and the Khmer temples. Fortunately, these can be combined at the nearby **Hang Pagoda**, also known as Ao Ban

Om, about 5 km south of town amd 300 m off the main road. It is not particularly special architecturally, but the sight of the hundreds of storks that rest in the grounds and wheel around the pointed roofs at dawn and dusk (1600-1800) is truly spectacular.

There's also the **Bao Tang Van Hoa Dan Toc Khmer** (0700-1100, 1300-1700) a small collection of artefacts next to the square-shaped lotus filled pond of Ba Om just south of town (there are plans for a hotel here). Labels are in Vietnamese and Khmer only; naga heads, Hanuman masks and musical instruments feature. Opposite is the **Chua Angkorajaborey (Ang)** or Chua Van Minh in Vietnamese dating from AD 990, which is rather peaceful.

Sa Dec → *For listings, see pages 78-84.*

Sa Dec's biggest claim to fame is that it was the birthplace of French novelist Marguerite Duras, and the town's three main avenues – Nguyen Hue, Tran Hung Dao and Hung Vuong garlanded with fragrant frangipani – together with some attractive colonial villas betray the French influence on this relatively young town. Sa Dec is also renowned for its flowers and bonsai trees. There are many flower nurseries on the fringes of the city. It is untouched by tourism and offers an untainted insight into life in one of the last attractive towns of the delta.

The town was formerly the capital of Dong Thap Province, a privilege that was snatched by Cao Lanh in 1984 but a responsibility that Sa Dec is better off without. It is a small and friendly town about 20 km west of Vinh Long. The delightful journey between the two towns passes brick kilns, and bikers transporting their wares (namely tropical fish in bottles and dogs).

Ins and outs
Getting there The most direct route is by crossing My Thuan Bridge and following the signs to Sa Dec. Local options include taxis, *Honda ôm* and sampans.

Tourist information There is no tourist information in Sa Dec. **Dong Thap Tourist Company** keeps some leaflets at the Sa Dec Hotel, and has a contact at the Huynh Thuy Le House (see below) but its main office is in Cao Lanh.

Sights
Sa Dec's bustling riverside market on Nguyen Hue Street is worth a visit. Many of the scenes from the film adaptation of Duras' novel *The Lover* were filmed in front of the shop terraces and merchants' houses here. Sit in one of the many riverside cafés to watch the world float by – which presumably, as a young woman, is what Duras did.

Duras' lover **Huynh Thuy Le's house** ① *Nha Co Huynh Thuy Le, 255A Nguyen Hue St, Ward 2, T67-377 3937, huynhthuyle@dongthaptourist.com, Mon-Sat 0730-1700, Sun 0830-1700, 10,000d,* is a lovely Sino-influenced building on the main street. There are stunning gold-leaf carved animal figures framing arches and the centrepiece is a golden shrine to Chinese warrior Quan Cong. The Ancient House was built in 1895 and restored in 1917. There are photographs of the Huynh family (he later married and had five daughters and three sons; he died in 1972), Duras and the Sa Dec school. The building was a police station and cared for from 1975-2006. The two friendly women who run the place, Xuan and Tuyen, speak French and English will offer you tea and crystallised ginger; this is a wonderful way to pass the afternoon. Reserved lunch and dinner are possible, as is a stay in the house. **Duras' childhood home** is not across the river as some guidebooks say; it no longer exists. She lived in a house near the Ecole de Sa Dec (now Truong Vuong

---

primary school on the corner of Hung Vuong and Ho Xuan Huong St), which is pictured inside the Nha Co Huynh Thuy Le.

Phuoc Hung Pagoda ① *75/5 Hung Vuong St*, is a splendid Chinese-style pagoda constructed in 1838 when Sa Dec was a humble one-road village. Surrounded by ornamental gardens, lotus ponds and cypress trees, the main temple to the right is decorated with fabulous animals assembled from pieces of porcelain rice bowls. Inside are some marvellous wooden statues of Buddhist figures made in 1838 by the venerable sculptor Cam. There are also some superbly preserved gilded wooden beams and two antique prayer tocsins. The smaller one was made in 1888 and its resounding mellow tone changes with the weather. The West Hall contains a valuable copy of the 101 volume Great Buddhist Canon. There are also some very interesting and ancient photos of dead devotees and of pagoda life in the past.

A few kilometres west of Sa Dec is the **Tu Ton Rose Garden (Vuon Hong Tu Ton)** ① *28 Vuon Hong St, Khom 3, Ward 3, T67-376 1685, 0600-2000, free*. The garden is next to a lemon yellow building with yellow gates. This 6000-ha nursery borders the river and is home to more than 40 varieties of rose and 540 other types of plant, from medicinal herbs to exotic orchids. Wander amid the potted hibiscus, beds of roses and bougainvillea and enjoy the visiting butterflies. The garden can be reached either on foot or by taking a *Honda ôm* to Tan Qui Don village.

Cao Lanh → *For listings, see pages 78-84.*

Cao Lanh for many years was a small, underdeveloped Mekong town. However, since becoming the capital of Dong Thap Province, an honour previously bestowed on Sa Dec, it has changed and has become a thriving market town. It also benefits from being the closest main city to, Xeo Quit base (Rung Cham forest), and Tram Chim Nature Reserve, all of which are main tourist attractions. In fact, the excursions are the only real reason to visit Cao Lanh, particularly if you are a bird lover or a Ho Chi Minh biographer.

Ins and outs
Getting there By car/bus from Ho Chi Minh City it is a three-hour drive. There are a few taxis, *Honda ôm*, river taxis and sampans.

Tourist information Dong Thap Tourist Co ① *2 Doc Binh Kieu St, T67-385 5637, www. dongthaptourist.com, Mon-Sat 0700-1130, 1330-1700*. Some staff have a reasonable command of English and are helpful and provide excellent value for the services it provides.

Sights
To the northeast along Nguyen Hue Street is the **war memorial**, containing the graves of Vietnamese who fell in the war with the USA. The **tomb of Ho Chi Minh's father** ① *Nguyen Sinh Sac (Tham Quan Khu Di Tich Nguyen Sinh Sac), next to Quan Nam restaurant at 137 Pham Huu Lau St, open 0700-1130, 1330-1700, 8000d*, set under a shell structure and sits in front of a lotus pond. A small stilt-house museum sits in the tranquil grounds.

The vast **Plain of Reeds (Dong Thap Muoi)** is a swamp that extends for miles north towards Cambodia, particularly in the late monsoon season (September to November). It is an important wildlife habitat (see below) but in the wet season, when the water levels rise, getting about on dry land can be a real problem. Extraordinarily, the Vietnamese have not adapted the stilt house solution used by the Khmer and every year get flooded out. In the rural districts houses are built on the highest land available and in a good year the floor will be just inches above the lapping water. At these times all transport is by boat. When the sky is grey the scene is desolate and the isolation of the plain can truly feel like the end of the Earth has been reached.

Tower Mound (Go Thap) is the best place from which to get a view of the immensity and beauty of the surrounding Plain of Reeds. There was a watchtower here although no one seems sure if it was 10-storeys high or the last in a chain of 10 towers. There are earthworks from which General Duong and Admiral Kieu conducted their resistance against the French between 1861 and 1866.

Tam Nong Bird Sanctuary (Tram Chim) is an 8000-ha reserve 45 km northwest of Cao Lanh (T67-382 7436). It contains 182 species of bird at various times of year, but most spectacular is the red-headed crane (sarus), rarest of the world's 15 crane species. Between August and November these spectacular creatures migrate across the nearby Cambodian border to avoid the floods (cranes feed on land), but at any other time, and particularly at dawn and dusk, they are a magnificent sight. Floating rice is grown in the area around the bird sanctuary and although the acreage planted diminishes each year this is another of nature's truly prodigious feats. The leaves float on the surface while the roots are anchored in mud as much as 4-5 m below; but as so much energy goes into growing the stalk little is left over for the ears of rice, so yields are low.

About 20 km east of Cao Lanh – 6 km off the main road at My Long where it is signposted to the on-site restaurant – **Xeo Quit Base** ① *T67-350 4733, kdtxeoquit@yahoo.com.vn, 0730-1700, 5000d for entrance and boat trip, Nguyen Thanh Nguyen is the only English-speaking guide at the site; T91-827 3125, he requires 1-2 days' notice.* Xeo Qiut was home to Viet Cong generals who planned the war from the safety of the base. There was so little vegetation cover here that fast-growing eucalyptus trees were planted; but even these took three years to provide sufficient cover to conceal humans. As the waterlogged ground prevented tunnelling, waterproof chambers sealed with plastic and resin were sunk into the mud. Stocked with rice, water and candles communist cadres coordinated their resistance strategy from here for almost 15 years. Despite frequent land and air raids the US forces never succeeded in finding or damaging the base. There is a restaurant at the site.

My Tho and around listings

For Sleeping and Eating price codes and other relevant information, see pages 10-13.

● Sleeping

My Tho *p70, map p71*

$$ Chuong Duong, No 10, 30 Thang 4 St, T730-387 0875, www.chuongduonghotel. com. My Tho's newest hotel occupies a prime riverside location in front of the erstwhile hydrofoil ferry. The staff are eager to please. All rooms are en suite, have a/c, satellite TV and minibar but are beginning to show their age. They also all overlook the river. The in-house restaurant provides good food.

$$ Minh Quan, 69 30 Thang 4 St, T730-397 9979, minhquanhotel@gmail.com. A new presence on the riverside road offering comfortable rooms with Wi-Fi and breakfast in a very convenient location.

$$ Song Tien, 33 Trung Trac St, T730-397 7883, www.tiengiangtourist.com. Undergone a remarkable transformation into a very nice 20-room hotel boasting large beds and bathtubs on legs. Price includes breakfast and now the best place in town.

$$ Song Tien 2, 101 Trung Trac St, T730-387 2009. This hotel was undergoing an extensive refurbishment in 2010.

$ Cong Doan, No 61, 30 Thang 4 St,

Mekong homestays

Facing Vinh Long town in the Co Chien River, a tributary of the Mekong, is a large island known as An Binh that is further sliced into smaller islands by ribbons of canals. **Cuu Long Tourist** runs several homestays on the island – a wonderful way to immerse yourself in local life.

The accommodation is basic with camp beds, shared bathrooms and mosquito nets and a home-cooked dinner of the fruits of the delta (elephant ear fish with abundant greens including mint and spring rolls and beef cooked in coconut). Sunset and drinks in patios or terraces or riverfront lookouts chatting with the owner completes the night. A dawn paddle in the Mekong, surrounded by floating water hyacinth and watching the sun rise is the reward for early risers. These tranquil islands are stuffed with fruit-bearing trees and flowers. Travel is by sampan or you can walk down the winding paths that link the communities. During your stay you will take tea and fruit at a traditional house, see rice cakes and popcorn being made, and visit a brick factory and watch terracotta pots being created close to the unusually shaped kilns that dot this area of the delta. Costs are US$49 per person or US$60 for two. Short of time? The four-hour tour costs US$25 for two people.

T730-387 4324, congdoantourist.tgg@vnn. vn. Clean hotel with 5 fan rooms that are cheaper than the 18 with a/c. Good views and location for the boat trips.

$ Rang Dong, No 25, 30 Thang 4 St, T730-387 4400, www.rangdonghotel.net. Private hotel, near river with a/c, TV and hot water.

$ Restaurant Hotel Rang Dong, 40/5, Section 3, ward 6, Le Thi Hong Gam St, T730-397 0085, www.rangdonghotel.net. About 1 km out of town on the riverfront but in an inconvenient location. This is the new sister hotel to the town centre **Rang Dong**. The best rooms are those with balconies overlooking the Mekong.

Ben Tre *p72*

$$ Hung Vuong, 148-166 Hung Vuong St, T75-382 2408. Spacious a/c rooms (39 in total) with huge bathtubs feature in this waterfront hotel that is in a great location. Each room has 2 beds plus TV, fridge and balcony. Restaurant; breakfast is included. Some English is spoken.

$ Cong Doan, 36 Hai Ba Trung St, T75-382 5082. All rooms with a/c, TV and bathrooms. No English spoken and much patience required at reception.

Vinh Long *p74*

For homestays, see box, above.

$$ Cuu Long (**B**), No 1, 1 Thang 5 St (ie No 1 May St), T70-382 3616, www. cuulongtourist.com. Set back from the river, in the centre of action. 34 comfortable a/c rooms; price includes breakfast (over the road at the **Phuy Thuong Restaurant**). The **Hoa Vien Club** in grounds next to the hotel is also good for a drink.

$ Nam Phuong, 11 Le Loi St, T70-382 2226, khachsannamphuongvl@yahoo.com. These comfortable rooms have a/c and hot water; clean and cheap and very friendly service. There's a big co-op mart nearby. Bikes to rent too.

$ Phung Hoang 1, 2H Hung Vuong St, T70-382 5185, ksphunghoang@yahoo.com. Very friendly service at this mini hotel. Clean rooms with varying facilities; cheaper rooms come with fan. Recommended.

$ Van Tram Nha Tro, No 4, 1 Thang 5 St, T70-382 3820. A small friendly place, close to the centre of the action, with 5 small and large a/c rooms with TV. Tours to An Binh offered that are cheaper than **Cuu Long Tourist** at US$24 for 2.

Tra Vinh *p75*

$$-$ Cuu Long, 999 Nguyen Thi Minh Khai St, T74-386 2615. About 2 km out of town, a modern hotel with a good choice of facilities. The rooms are well equipped with a/c, satellite TV, and en suite facilities. The restaurant provides a good selection of food at reasonable prices. The friendly, helpful staff have a good understanding of English. Although it is 2 km from town if you are planning to stay overnight in Tra Vinh then this hotel is recommended. Wi-Fi and breakfast included.

$ Duy Thanh, 6 Dien Bien Phu St, T74-385 8034. Diagonally opposite the market and main roundabout. Windowless rooms smell and so it's worth forking out the extra 80,000d for a window and some air. Friendly reception.

$ Tra Vinh Palace, 3 Le Thanh To St, T74-386 4999. A comfortable and quiet hotel with very large rooms 10 mins' walk from the central market. Staff are helpful. Wi-Fi available. The sister hotel, **Tra Vinh Palace 2** has cheaper rooms (**$**) and is a few streets away.

Sa Dec *p76*

$$ Nha Co Huynh Thuy Le, 255A Nguyen Hue St, Ward 2, T67-377 3937. Run by **Dong Thap Tourist**, this lovely home has 4 fan rooms with 2 single beds in each and would be the most enjoyable way to spend time in Sa Dec. The 2 front rooms are much more attractive than the plain 2 back rooms with stained-glass windows and carved wooden doors. The shared bathroom is at the back with cold water. The price includes breakfast and dinner. See also Eating, below.

$$-$ Bong Hong, 251A Nguyen Sinh Sac St, T67-386 8287, bonghonghotel@yahoo.com.vn. A short distance before the bus station on Highway 80 leading into town. Some good-value a/c rooms with TV and fridge. Cheaper rooms have fan and cold water only. Breakfast not included. Tennis court on site.

$$-$ Sa Dec, 108/5A (499) Hung Vuong St, T67-386 1430, sadechotel@yahoo.com.vn.

More expensive rooms come equipped with a/c, hot water, TV and a fridge; cheaper ones make do with a fan and warm water showers. Somewhat run down and unloved but clean. Breakfast included except for fan rooms. Closer to the river than the **Bong Hong**.

Cao Lanh *p77*

$$$-$ Song Tra, 178 Nguyen Hue St, T67-385 2624, www.dongthaptourist.com. Cao Lanh's best hotel with a good location in the town. The rooms are tastefully decorated and come equipped with a/c, satellite TV and en suite facilities. The staff are helpful and friendly, with a decent grasp of English. The restaurant is reasonable. See Eating, below.

$$-$ Hoa Binh, east of town on Highway 30 towards My Tho, opposite the striking war memorial, T67-385 1469. All a/c, some nice rooms. Friendly and helpful staff. The rooms come equipped with a/c, phone, satellite TV, minibar and en suite facilities. The restaurant on the ground floor provides a reasonable selection of food. If it were not for the fact that it is a little way out of town it would be the best hotel. Wi-Fi available.

$ Binh Minh Hotel, 157 Hung Vuong St, T67-385 3423. A good little hotel but note that it's actual entrance is not on Hung Vuong, it is just around the corner from the Vespa/Piaggio garage on Do Cong Tuong St. The owner, a local schoolteacher, is friendly and helpful. If you are travelling on a budget then this would be a good choice. Fan and a/c rooms.

$ Xuan Mai, 33 Le Quy Don St, T67-385 2852. Clean and spacious hotel; all rooms with a/c, fridge and bath but breakfast is not included. One of the better restaurants in town. The staff are friendly and helpful, the rooms tastefully decorated and there's internet and Wi-Fi access.

● Eating

My Tho *p70, map p71*
A speciality of the area is *hu tieu my tho*, a

spicy soup of vermicelli, sliced pork, dried shrimps and fresh herbs. Sadly most of the good cheap restaurants have been cleared away from **Trung Trac St** but some remain. At night noodle stalls spring up on the pavement of **Le Loi St** by the junction with Le Dai Han.

† **Banh Xeo 46**, 11 Trung Trac St. Serves *bánh xèo*, savoury pancakes filled with beansprouts, mushrooms and prawns; delicious.
† **Hu Tieu 44**, 44 Nam Ky Khoi Nghia St. 0500-1200. Specializes in *hu tieu my tho*. At 16,000d for a good-sized bowl filled to the top with *hu tieu my tho*, it is unbeatable.
† **Hu Tieu Chay 24**, 24 Nam Ky Khoi Nghia St. It is the vegetarian equivalent of **Hu Tieu 44** and is even cheaper than the meat variety.
† **Lac Hong**, 63, 30 Thang 4 St, is the latest place to be seen. Sip your coffee in the cool and watch the world go by.

Ben Tre *p72*
Most of the hotels have restaurants; there is a floating restaurant on the river but it has moved from its town centre location to 1 km upstream because, they say, it's a prettier location; not so. The best option is local noodle and rice stands. The hotel restaurants are open all day. The choice is adequate.
† **Dong Khoi Hotel**, see Sleeping, above. The restaurant, next to the hotel, has a good selection. English spoken.
† **Nha Hang Noi Ben Tre**, Hung Vuong, T75-382 2492. 0700-2200. A variety of dishes plus karaoke on this large boat overlooking the banks of the river in its new location. It's not within walking distance.

Vinh Long *p74*
It is remarkably difficult to find anything to eat in Vinh Long apart from the bountiful fruit in the market. There are a few restaurants along 1 Thang 5 St, just beyond **Cuu Long Hotel** (A).
† **Nem Nuong**, 12 1 Thang 5 St. Open all day. Sells grilled meat with noodles.
† **Phuong Thuy Restaurant**, No 1, 1 Thang 5 St, T70-382 4786. 0600-2100. A 'stilt'

restaurant on the river with Vietnamese and Western dishes and welcoming service. Cuttlefish and shrimp feature strongly.

Cafés
Hoa Nang Cafe, 1 Thang 5 St. A great spot for a sunset drink, and for morning coffee when it is exceptionally busy.

Tra Vinh *p75*
† **Cuu Long**, see Sleeping, above. Restaurant has a good selection of food.
† **Tuy Huong**, 8 Dien Bien Phu St. Opposite the market; good, simple Vietnamese dishes.
† **Viet Hoa**, 80 Tran Phu St. Walk through the garage to sample the squid, shrimp and crab dishes. English menu.

Sa Dec *p76*
† **Cay Sung**, 2/4 Hung Vuong St. Open all day. It serves a good selection of rice dishes. The *duong chau* (fried rice) in particular is good. There is a menu in English available. The food is well presented and piping hot.
† **Thuy Com**, 439 Hung Vuong St, T67-386 1644. Serves excellent *dong chau*. The menu is in English and there is a variety of food.
† **Nha Co Huynh Thuy Le**, 255A Nguyen Hue St, Ward 2, T67-377 3937. Run by **Dong Thap Tourist**, reserve a day in advance for the chance to dine in the home of Marguerite Duras' lover. Attended to by Xuan and Tuyen who are guides at the house, dine on spring rolls, fried fish, lotus salad, noodles, fried vegetables with pork and fruit. Lunch and dinner menus are US$6 each for 5 courses.

Cao Lanh *p77*
The restaurants in Song Tra, Xuan Mai and Hoa Binh hotels are all open for breakfast, lunch and dinner. There is not much difference in their quality, presentation choice and value. The highlight, however, is the attractively presented weekend buffet in the **Song Tra Hotel** garden (see Sleeping, above), on Sat and Sun nights.
† **A Chau**, Ly Thuong Kiet St. 0800-2100. Specializes in fried pancakes.

Hong Nhien, 143 Hung Vuong St, behind the Song Tra Hotel. Serves *com tam* and *hu tieu* in a simple set up.

🛍 Shopping

Ben Tre *p72*
The main items to buy are coconuts and related coconut-made products. They might not be too versatile but they are very pretty and make ideal novelty presents for friends and family at home. The gift cabinet in the **Dong Khoi** hotel has the best selection of coconut-related items.

⛰ Activities and tours

My Tho *p70, map p71*
Tour operators
Ben Tre Tourist, 8, 30 Thang 4 St, T730-387 5070, www.bentretourist.vn. Although this company operates island tours from My Tho, it would be best to use its specialist knowledge of Ben Tre province. Escape the My Tho crowds with homestays at Cai Mon and take a tour to the gardens and canals of this neigbouring province.
Chuong Duong Tourist, next to the hotel, T730-387 0875, cdhoteltravel@vnn.vn. Offers the same tour as **Tien Giang Tourist** for the same price but for 3 hrs.
Tien Giang Tourist, Dockside location is at No 8, 30 Thang 4 St, T730-387 3184, www.tiengiangtourist.com. Dinner with traditional music on the Mekong for US$28. Canoe hire is US$50 per hr for 2 people and a boat is US$12 for 1½ hrs.

Ben Tre *p72*
Tour operators
Tours of the islands in the Tien River from Ben Tre cost half the price of those leaving from My Tho and include taking a horse and cart. The 4-hr Ben Tre ecological tour will take you to see local agricultural industries.
Ben Tre Tourist, 16 Hai Ba Trung St, T75-382 2392, www.bentretourist.vn. Daily 0700-1100, 1300-1700. Island tour, US$8 for 2; Ben Tre ecological tour, US$11 for 2. Bicycles can be rented for US$0.60 per hr or US$1.90 per day. There's also a motorboat for rent for US$5.60 per hr.

Vinh Long *p74*
Tour operators
Cuu Long Tourist, No 1, 1 Thang 5 St, T70-382 3616, www.cuulongtourist.com. Trips to An Binh Island include a visit to the floating market of Cai Be. A tour of the area including homestay, dinner and breakfast can be arranged (see box, page 79). A day trip to Cai Be passing the floating market, is possible as is the arrangement from HCMC.
Mekong Travel, No 8, 30 Thang 5 St, T70-383 6252, www.mekongtravel.com.vn. Breaking the monopoly of **Cuu Long Tourist** is this new company offering the same homestay and floating market options.

Tra Vinh *p75*
Tra Vinh Tourist, 64-66 Le Loi St, T74-385 8556, travinhtourist@yahoo.com.

Sa Dec *p76*
Dong Thap Tourist, is based at the Huynh Thuy Le Old House, T67-377 3937, www.dongthaptourist.com. Trips to Xeo Quit and Cao Lanh organized.

Cao Lanh *p77*
Birdwatching at the nearby sanctuaries is the most common activity. It is also possible to hire boats from **Dong Thap Tourist Company**, 2 Doc Binh Kieu St, T67-385 5637. Dong Thap also organizes trips to the mausoleum of Nguyen Sinh Sac, Xeo Quit, Sa Dec and the Gao Giong Eco-tourism Zone.

⊖ Transport

My Tho *p70, map p71*
Boat
As in all Mekong Delta towns, local travel is often by boat to visit the orchards, islands and remoter places.

Bus

Local On land there are *xe ôms*.

Long distance The bus station (**Ben Xe My Tho**) is 3-4 km from town on Ap Bac St towards HCMC with regular connections every 30 mins from 0430 to **HCMC**'s Mien Tay station (2 hrs); **Vinh Long** (2½ hrs); and **Cao Lanh** (2½ hrs). There are also buses to **Can Tho** and **Chau Doc**.

Ben Tre *p72*
Car

Ben Tre is 70 km from **My Tho**, 32 km from **Can Tho**, and 147 km from **HCMC** via the My Thuan toll bridge. It is possible to travel from Ben Tre to **Vinh Long** along route 60 then 57, which takes 1 hr to the ferry crossing from Long Ho (15,000d). This tarmacked route passes plenty of small bridges and village life.

Vinh Long *p74*
Bus

The local bus station is on 3 Thang 2 St, between Hung Dao Vuong and Hung Vuong in the centre of town with services to Sa Dec and Can Tho. The long-distance bus station is at Dinh Tien Hoang St, Ward 8 for connections with **HCMC**'s Mien Tay station. Links with **My Tho**, **Long Xuyen**, Tra Vinh, **Rach Gia**, and other Mekong Delta destinations.

Tra Vinh *p75*
Bus

The bus station is on Nguyen Dang St, about 500 m south of town. Regular connections with **Vinh Long**.

Sa Dec *p76*
Bus

The bus station is about 500 m southeast of town on the main road just before the bridge. Buses to **Vinh Long** and **Long Xuyen** leave from here. The town is 143 km from HCMC and 102 km from Chau Doc, and 20 km from Vinh Long along Highway 80.

Taxi

Vina Taxi, T67-386 6666.

Cao Lanh *p77*
Bus

The bus station is located at the corner of Ton That Tung and Doc Binh Kieu St. Connections with all delta towns. To **HCMC** from the bus station on Vo Thi Sau St and Nguyen Van Troi St.

Directory

My Tho *p70, map p71*
Banks EXIM, Le Van Duyet St, T730-387 9374. Offers a bureau de change service as does the **Incombank**, on Nam Ky Khoi Nghia St. There's also a Visa and Plus ATM at the Truong Luong Restaurant just outside My Tho that is used by tour operators and ATMs on 30 Thang 4 St. **BIDV** ATM next to the post office. **Hospitals** 2 Hung Vuong St, T730-387 2360. **Internet** The post office and Choung Dong hotel offer internet and there's Wi-Fi at the Lac Hong café. **Post office** 2 Truong Dinh St. Facilities for international telephone calls, 0700-1130, 1330-1700.

Ben Tre *p72*
Banks Cong Thuong Bank, 142 Nguyen Dinh Chieu St, T75-382 2507. It offers a bureau de change service and cashes TCs. **Agribank**, on the corner of Le Lai and Dong Khoi St, has a Visa ATM. **Hospitals** Nguyen Dinh Chieu Hospital, 109 Doan Hoang Minh St. **Post office** 3 Dong Khoi St, T75-382 2264, 0700-1100, 1300-1700. It also has internet access.

Vinh Long *p74*
Banks Agribank, 47 1 Thang 5 St. With ATM. There's a Visa ATM next to the Cuu Long B hotel. **Hospitals** 301 Tran Phu St, Ward 4, T70-382 3520. **Internet** The post office and Cuu Long (B) offer internet access and there are a couple of email places on Ly Thuong Kiet St. **Post office** 12c Hoang Thai Hieu St, T70-382 5888. 0600-2100.

Tra Vinh *p75*
Banks Vietinbank, 15A Dien Binh Phu St,

has a bureau de change service and also cash advances off Visa and MasterCard. ATM too. **Sacombank**, 40 Dien Bien Phu St with ATM. **Hospitals** 27 Dien Binh Phu, Ward 6, T74-386 2458. **Internet** At the post office and 83 Le Loi St. **Post office** Corner of Hung Vuong St and Ngo Quyen St has internet.

Sa Dec *p76*
Banks Agribank, 77 Ly Thuong Kiet St, off Tran Hung Dao St. **Sacombank**, 6-7Nguyen Sinh Sac St. **Hospitals** Ap Hoa Khanh, Ward 2, T67-386 1964. **Post office** 90 Hung Vuong St, Ward 2, T67-386 1025. Internet service.

Cao Lanh *p77*
Banks Vietinbank, corner of Nguyen Hue and Ly Thuong Kiet St with ATM. **Sacombank**, 43 Ly Thuong Kiet St. **Hospitals** Dong Thap Hospital, Ap 3 Xa My Tan Thi Xa Cao Lanh, T67-385 1130. **Internet** Xuan Mai hotel. **Post office** 83-85 Nguyen Hue St, T67-389 8989.

Can Tho and around

Can Tho is a large and rapidly growing commercial city situated in the heart of the Mekong Delta. Lying chiefly on the west bank of the Can Tho River it is the capital of Can Tho Province, the largest city in the delta, and the region's principal transport hub, with roads and canals running to most other important towns. It is also one of the most welcoming of the delta towns and is the launch pad for trips to see some of the region's floating markets. South of Can Tho are the towns of Soc Trang, Bac Lieu and Ca Mau. ⟿ *For listings, see pages 90-95.*

Can Tho → *For listings, see pages 90-95.*

A small settlement was established at Can Tho at the end of the 18th century, although the town did not prosper until the French took control of the Delta a century later and rice production for export began to take off. Despite the city's rapid recent growth there are still strong vestiges of French influence apparent in the broad boulevards flanked by flame trees, as well as many elegant buildings. Can Tho was also an important US base. Paul Theroux in *The Great Railway Bazaar* wrote: "Can Tho was once the home of thousands of GIs. With the brothels and bars closed, it had the abandoned look of an unused fairground after a busy summer. In a matter of time, very few years, there will be little evidence that the Americans were ever there. There are poisoned rice fields between the straggling fingers of the Mekong Delta and there are hundreds of blond and fuzzy-haired children, but in a generation even these unusual features will change."

Ins and outs

Getting there Virtually all visitors arrive by road. With the My Thuan Bridge (near Vinh Long) and the new bridge linking Vinh Long and Can Tho, journey times have fallen. ⟿ *See Transport, page 94.*

Getting around Quite a lot of Can Tho can be explored on foot. *Xe lôi* the Mekong cyclo is no longer able to trade between 0600-1800 due to traffic problems but a motorbike taxi can be picked up. Some of the sites, the floating markets for instance, are best visited by boat. There are also river taxis and an efficient public bus service.

Best time to visit As in all the other Mekong cities the best time is from December to April when the temperatures are warm and there is no rain. May to November is the monsoon season and as such it is prone to flooding (although it does fare better than other cities).

Background Can Tho has its own university, founded in 1966 and also a famous rice research institute, located at O Mon, 25 km away on Highway 91. Like the **International Rice Research Institute** (IRRI), its more famous counterpart at Los Baños in the Philippines (and to which it is attached), one of the Can Tho institute's key functions is developing rice hybrids that will flourish in the varied conditions of the delta. Near the coast, rice has to be tolerant of salt and tidal flooding. In Dong Thap Province, near Cambodia, floating rice grows stalks of 4-5 m in order to keep its head above the annual flood. The task of the agronomists is to produce varieties which flourish in these diverse environments and at the same time produce decent yields.

Sights

Hai Ba Trung Street, alongside the river, is the heart of the town; at dusk families stroll in the park here in their Sunday best. Opposite the park is **Chua Ong Pagoda** ① *34 Hai Ba Trung St*, dating from 1894 and built by Chinese from Guangzhou. Unusually for a Chinese temple it is not free-standing but part of a terrace of buildings. The right-hand side of the pagoda is dedicated to the Goddess of Fortune, while the left-hand side belongs to General Ma Tien, who, to judge from his unsmiling statue, is fierce and warlike and not to be trifled with. The layout is a combination of typical pagoda – with

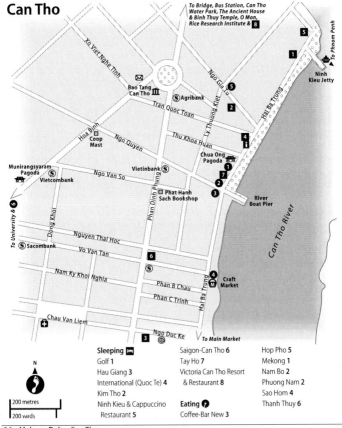

Can Tho

To Bridge, Bus Station, Can Tho Water Park, The Ancient House & Binh Thuy Temple, O Mon, Rice Research Institute & 8

To Phnom Penh

Ninh Kieu Jetty

Xo Viet Nghe Tinh
Ngo Gia Tu
Ly Thuong Kiet
Hai Ba Trung
Bao Tang Can Tho
Agribank
Tran Quoc Toan
Thu Khoa Huan
Hoa Binh
Coop Mast
Ngo Quyen
Chua Ong Pagoda
Munirangsyaram Pagoda
Vietcombank
Vietinbank
Ngo Van So
Phan Dinh Phung
Phat Hanh Sach Bookshop
River Boat Pier
Dong Khoi
Nguyen Thai Hoc
Vo Van Tan
Sacombank
Nam Ky Khoi Nghia
Phan B Chau
Phan C Trinh
Hai Ba Trung
Craft Market
Chau Van Liem
Ngo Duc Ke
To Main Market
Can Tho River
To University & 6

N
200 metres
200 yards

Sleeping 🛏
Golf 1
Hau Giang 3
International (Quoc Te) 4
Kim Tho 2
Ninh Kieu & Cappuccino Restaurant 5

Saigon-Can Tho 6
Tay Ho 7
Victoria Can Tho Resort & Restaurant 8

Eating 🍴
Coffee-Bar New 3

Hop Pho 5
Mekong 1
Nam Bo 2
Phuong Nam 2
Sao Hom 4
Thanh Thuy 6

a small open courtyard for the incense smoke to escape – and typical meeting house, complete with its language school, of the overseas Chinese in Southeast Asia.

The bustling market that used to operate on Hai Ba Trung Street along the bank of the river, and gave the town a bit of character, has been moved 1 km downriver. A new riverside promenade has been created. There's also a new crafts market building with a riverside restaurant, see Eating, page 92.

The **Munirang-syaram Pagoda** ① *36 Hoa Binh Blvd (southwest of post office)*, was built just after the Vietnam War and is a Khmer Hinayana Buddhist sanctuary. **Bao Tang Can Tho** ① *Hoa Binh St, Tue-Thu 0800-1100, 1400-1700, Sat-Sun 0800-1100, 1830-2100*, in an impressive building, is the local history museum.

The **Can Tho Water Park** (**Cong Vien Nuoc Can Tho**) ① *near the Hotel Victoria Can Tho at Tran Van Kheu, T710-376 3343, Mon-Fri 0845-1800, Sat-Sun 0740-1900, 40,000d*, provides liquid fun on slides and in pools.

Binh Thuy Temple, 7 km north along the road to Long Xuyen, dates from the mid-19th century; festivals are held here in the middle of the fourth and 12th lunar months. Nearby, 500 m down Bui Huu Nghia Road, opposite Binh Thuy temple, visit **Nha Co Binh Thuy** aka the **ancient house** ① *10,000d to go inside the house; ask the owners,* (also known as Vuon Lan if you get a moto to take you there), which was used as a setting in the film *The Lover*.

Floating markets

① *The daily markets are busiest at around 0600-0900. Women with sampans to rent will approach travellers in Hai Ba Trung St near the market waving a book of testimonials from previous satisfied customers. Expect to pay about US$15 for 2 people for 3 hrs. Set off as early as possible to beat the flotilla of tour boats. A trip of at least 5 hrs is recommended to see the landscape at a leisurely pace. If you take a larger boat you will not be able to manoeuvre in and out of the market.*

There are boat trips to the floating markets at **Phung Hiep**, 33 km away (an eight-hour round trip by sampan or take a bus to Phung Hiep and rent a boat there) and **Phong Dien**, 15 km down the Can Tho River (a five-hour trip). **Cai Rang** is 7 km away and is easy to visit for those with only a couple of hours to spare. Bustling affairs, the vendors attach a sample of their wares to a bamboo pole to attract customers. Up to seven vegetables can be seen dangling from staffs – wintermelon, pumpkin, spring onions, giant parsnips, grapefruit, garlic, mango, onions and Vietnamese plums. Housewives paddle their sampans from boat to boat and barter, haggle and gossip in the usual way. At the back of the boats, the domesticity of life on the water is in full glare – washing is hung out and motors are stranded high above the water.

Phung Hiep also features yards making traditional fishing boats and rice barges. Orchards and gardens abound, small sampans are best as they can negotiate the narrowest canals to take the visitor into the heart of the area, a veritable Garden of Eden.

Soc Trang → *For listings, see pages 90-95.*

Soc Trang is a large, sprawling and scruffy town which sits astride a narrow branch of the Mekong and is dominated by a huge telecommunications mast. The town is home to a large Khmer community, as is witnessed by the darker skin of many of its inhabitants. Indeed, most of its attraction lies in this connection and for those running to a leisurely timetable it might warrant a visit, which can be done as a day trip from Can Tho.

On the 14th-15th day of the 10th lunar month (around late November or early December) the town dusts itself down and generates a carnival atmosphere for the lively **Oc Om Boc Festival** with its Nho boat racing. People come from miles around to watch Khmer boats racing on the river, with hundreds of young men paddling furiously. The event is an echo of the Phnom Penh boat festival that celebrates the turning of the waters when water in the Tonlé Sap branch of the Mekong reverses its flow and backs up into the Tonlé Sap Lake.

Ins and outs

Getting there The most direct route is to head to Can Tho and then follow the signs along Highway 1A. ▸▸ *See Transport, page 94.*

Best time to visit December to April is the best time to visit but if possible try and plan your trip to coincide with the festival.

Tourist information Soc Trang Tourist ① *131 Nguyen Chi Thanh St, T79-382 2292, www.soctrangtourism.com.*

History

Soc Trang, along with its neighbours of Tra Vinh and Bac Lieu is home to many Khmer and Chinese. Soc Trang and Bac Lieu have the largest concentrations of Khmer in Vietnam. The city was founded in the late 1700s. Many of the stunning temples date from the early 1800s.

Sights

At the top end of town on Nguyen Thi Minh Khai Street is the **Kleang Pagoda**, a temple built in traditional Cambodian style, perched on a two-level terrace. Vivid colours adorn the windows and doors while inside sits a fine golden Sakyamuni statue. Opposite the pagoda is the **Khmer Museum** ① *Mon-Sat 0730-1100, 1330-1700, free,* in which musical instruments, traditional clothing and agricultural tools form the rather uninspired display.

About 3 km out of town (follow Le Hong Phong Street and fork right after the fire station) is the **Matoc Pagoda** or **Chua Doi** (or Maha Tup as it is properly called in Khmer). The main pagoda is on the right and is decorated with superb, brightly coloured murals; it has been restored with donations from the Vietnamese and Khmer diaspora. Buddhists have worshipped on this holy site for over 400 years, but the pagoda's current incarnation is relatively modern. The chief attraction of the place, megachirop- teraphobes excepted, is the fruit bat. Thousands of these enormous mammals roost in the trees behind the pagoda and at dusk are an impressive sight as they fly off en masse to find food, literally blackening the sky. Also behind the pagoda are the monks' living quarters and the tombs of some five-toed pigs, which have special significance for this community. Look carefully at the picture on the grave!

Bac Lieu → *For listings, see pages 90-95.*

Bac Lieu is a small and pretty riverside city and the provincial capital of Bac Lieu Province. It is not as rich in rice production as other Mekong provinces on account of its proximity to the sea, so the enterprizing locals have salt farms instead. They also make a living out of oysters and fishing. New hotels and buildings are being erected and they are trying to capture some of the lucrative Tra Vinh market (there are many Khmer living here and several temples). Bac Lieu has a bird sanctuary that has large numbers of white herons.

Ins and outs

Getting there It is 56 km from Soc Trang, 113 km from Can Tho, 287 km from Ho Chi Minh City and 67 km from Ca Mau. The roads have improved but it is a long drive. ⏵ *See Transport, page 94.*

Tourist information Bac Lieu Tourist Company ⓘ *2 Hoang Van Thu St, T781-382 4272, www.baclieutourist.com*, has a reasonable selection of quite moderately priced tours and is eager to help but only basic English is spoken. The office is closed Saturday afternoons and Sundays.

History

The earliest inhabitants were part of the Funan Empire (see Oc-Eo, page 101). There is a Cham Stupa dating from AD 892 in Vinh Hung. It is somewhat overgrown with vegetation but if you are in the neighbourhood it is quite interesting. Life has always been hard in the province due to saltwater intrusion.

Sights

The **bird sanctuary**, 3 km southwest of town, is home to a large white heron population. The best times to visit are December and January. The birds nest in January and then migrate and do not return until late May. Do apply plenty of mosquito repellent as the place is inundated with biting insects.

Xiem Can Temple (Komphir Sakor Prekchru) ⓘ *12 km west of Bac Lieu, free to enter but alms would be appreciated*, is a pretty Khmer temple complex. It was built in 1887 and a small group of monks still resides here.

Hoi Binh Moi Temple (Resay Vongsaphuth lethmay) is one of the newer temples as it was constructed in 1952. A recent addition (1990) is the ossuary tower. There is a small monastic school attached to the temple.

Ca Mau → *For listings, see pages 90-95.*

Ca Mau is the provincial capital of Ca Mau Province, Vietnam's most southerly province and is a huge, ugly, cluttered urban sprawl. The province consists primarily of the U Minh cajeput forest and swamp, both of which are the largest in Vietnam. Right at the tip of the country is the new Mui Ca Mau National Park. Apart from a reasonable selection of churches and pagodas Ca Mau's main interest is for botanists and ornithologists.

Ins and outs

Getting there and around There are seasonal direct flights from Ho Chi Minh City, bus connections and a boat from Rach Gia. The city has plenty of taxis and river taxis and a public bus service. ⏵ *See Transport, page 94.*

Best time to visit This is somewhat complex as in the dry season U Minh Forest is liable to forest fires and the whole area is very dry. In the monsoon season flooding occurs on a regular basis. December to February should be the best months to visit.

Tourist information Minh Hai Tourist ⓘ *91 Phan Dinh Phung St, T780-383 1828, www.dulichminhhai.com, Mon-Fri 0730-1100, 1330-1700, Sat 0730-1100*, is a well-run and professional travel agency offering the full spectrum of services. Very little English is spoken.

History

The first attempt at cultivation was in the 17th century. It has been on and off ever since. The main problems facing those trying to cultivate the area is the presence of the saline swamp and mangrove forest. Fishing is still the mainstay of the local economy. The U Minh Forest was a favoured hiding place for the Viet Cong troops during the war. A large quantity of chemical defoliant was dropped to destroy the forest. Eucalyptus trees were planted as they proved resilient to Agent Orange and other defoliants.

Sights

A **Cao Dai Temple** is located on Phan Ngoc Hien street. Although not as large as the main one in Tay Ninh it is still an impressive structure. It houses quite a few monks and is thriving. The monks will be happy to explain Cao Daism.

The **U Minh Forest** is the main reason most people visit Ca Mau. The U Minh Forest was a favoured hiding place for the Viet Cong troops during the war. Despite the chemical damage and the huge postwar deforestation to make way for shrimp farms there are still trees and large numbers of birds to be seen and it is a favourite destination for ornithologists. It is also of interest to botanists. **Minh Hai Tourist** operates an all-day tour of the forest and mangrove swamps for US$52 per person including tour guide, car and ticket. Note that tours may be off limits from May to October due to forest fires.

The **Mui Ca Mau National Park**, at the southern edge of the country, has been named a UNESCO World Biosphere Reserve. The 41,862-ha park of mangrove and mudflats is home to hundreds of animals and birds. Some of the birds include the Far Eastern curlew, Chinese egret, and black-headed ibis. **Minh Hai Tourist** arranges tours for US$73 for two including tour guide, speedboat and ticket.

Can Tho and around listings

For Sleeping and Eating price codes and other relevant information, see pages 10-13.

● Sleeping

Can Tho *p85, map p86*

$$$$ Victoria Can Tho Resort, Cai Khe ward, T710-381 0111, www.victoriahotels. asia. A 92-room riverside hotel set in lovely, well- tended garden on its own little peninsula. It is Victoria Hotel 'French colonial' style at its best with a breezy open reception area and emphasis on comfort and plenty of genuine period features. It has a pool, spa pavilion, tennis court and restaurant. The staff are multilingual and helpful. The a/c rooms are well decorated and have satellite TV, Wi-Fi, en suite facilities, decent-sized bathtub, well-stocked minibar and electronic safe in the room. Even if you decide to stay in a more centrally and somewhat cheaper hotel then a visit to the grounds and one of the restaurants would be a pleasant experience. The hotel offers a complimentary boat shuttle to the town centre.

$$$$ Golf Hotel, 2 Hai Ba Trung St, T710-381 2210, www.vinagolf.vn. No longer the tallest hotel in town with its 10 floors. The services and facilities are on a par with the better hotels in HCMC and Hanoi but it always seems empty. The staff are friendly. The rooms are well equipped with all mod cons en suite. The restaurants provide fine dining and the views from the **Windy Sky Bar** (8th floor) are superb. The swimming 'fool' on site is a draw. ATM on site.

$$$-$$ Kim Tho, 14 Ngo Gia Tu St, T710-322 2228, www.kimtho.com. The closest thing to boutique hotel in the delta with low-slung beds and white linens. Don't bother paying extra for a room with a views.

Choose a standard with a bathtub. The standout attraction is the roof-top café with fabulous views. Includes breakfast.

$$$-$$ Ninh Kieu, 2 Hai Ba Trung St, T710-382 1171, www.ninhkieuhotel.vn. Lovely position on the river and a popular venue, in the wedding season for Can Tho's classier wedding receptions. Parts of the hotel have undergone renovation; there are now 97 rooms, 3 floating restaurants, a bar, tennis courts and sauna. The rooms have a/c and en suite facilities and those in the older, unrenovated building are cheaper (buildings A1 and A2). Rooms in A3 are large and comfortable. The staff are friendly.

$$$-$$ Saigon-Can Tho, 55 Phan Dinh Phung St, T710-382 5831, www.saigoncantho.com.vn. A/c, comfortable, central business hotel in the competent hands of **Saigontourist**. The staff are friendly and helpful. The rooms are well equipped with a/c, satellite TV, en suite facilities and minibar. There's a currency exchange, free internet and Wi-Fi for guests, sauna and breakfast included.

$$ International (Quoc Te), 12 Hai Ba Trung St, T710-382 2079, http://canthotourist.vn. This hotel, heavy in appearance, overlooks the river with a good if rather soulless restaurant. The a/c rooms are somewhat drab and a coat of paint would not go amiss on the outside. But, that being said, the rooms are large and reasonably equipped with satellite TV and en suite facilities; bathrooms have tubsl. Breakfast and Wi-Fi included.

$ Tay Ho, 42 Hai Ba Trung St, T710-382 3392, tay_ho@hotmail.com. This lovely place has a variety of rooms and a great public balcony that can be enjoyed by those paying for back rooms. All rooms now have private bathrooms. River view rooms, inevitably, cost more. The staff are friendly.

$ Hau Giang, 27 Chau Van Liem St, T710-382 1950. 70 a/c rooms all with hot water, TV and fridge. Breakfast and Wi-Fi is included. Used by backpacker tour groups from HCMC, good value. No English spoken.

Soc Trang *p87*

$ Khanh Hung, 15 Tran Hung Dao St, T79-382 1026. A/c and fan rooms, hot water, satellite TV, some very nice rooms, friendly; restaurant on the premises. Recommended. No English spoken.

$ Phong Lan, 124 Dong Khoi St, T79-382 1619. A/c, hot water, some rooms have a balcony overlooking the river.

$ Phong Lan 2, 133 Nguyen Chi Thanh St, T79-382 1757. Reasonable hotel, next to **Soc Trang Tourist**, offering comfortable rooms with Wi-Fi and TV. Restaurant also. Some English spoken.

Bac Lieu *p88*

$$-$ Bac Lieu Hotel, 4-6 Hoang Van Thu St, T781-382 2437, baclieuhotel@yahoo.com. A good little 3-star hotel. The location is central, near the river. The rooms are reasonably well equipped with a/c, satellite TV and en suite facilities. The staff are friendly and helpful. English is spoken. The restaurant has a reasonable selection on offer and is cheap.

$$-$ Cong Tu Bac Lieu, 13 Dien Bien Phu St, T781-395 3304. A stunning French colonial home that has undergone a sprucing up. Its ochre front with duck egg blue shutters looks out over the river. There's fanciful stucco work and beautiful tiling throughout. Linger in the café or the restaurant compound behind. ATM on site.

Ca Mau *p89*

$$-$ Quoc Te, 179 Phan Ngoc Hien St, T780-366 6666, www.hotelquocte.com. The pick of the bunch for the Ca Mau hotels. They have nice rooms to cater for all budgets. The staff are very friendly and helpful and speak good English. The facilities include Wi-Fi and a restaurant that closes at 2200 serving Western and Vietnamese food.

$$-$ Hoang Gia, 27-29 Tran Hung Dao St, ward 5, T780-381 9999. A clean, quiet and pleasant hotel.

$ Ca Mau Hotel, 20 Phan Ngoc Hien St, T780-383 1165. All the rooms have a/c and are pleasantly equipped with en suite facilities. Good location, modern and the staff are friendly and helpful. The restaurant is open all day and is reasonable. Some English is spoken.

$ Song Hung Hotel, 28 Phan Ngoc Hien St, T780-382 2822. Good location. Plesant modern rooms with en suite and a/c. Helpful staff but no English spoken.

$ Quoc Nam, 23 Phan Boi Chau St, T780-382 7514. Charming little hotel with an excellent café on top offering great views of Ca Mau. Good value for money. Helpful staff but cars may have difficulty pulling up because of the narrow road by the river.

🍴 Eating

Can Tho *p85, map p86*
Hai Ba Trung St by the river offers a good range of excellent and very well-priced little restaurants, and the riverside setting is an attractive one.

🍴🍴-🍴 Victoria Can Tho Spices, see Sleeping, above. Excellent location on the river bank where it's possible to dine alfresco or inside its elegant restaurant. The food is delicious and the service is excellent. Try the deep-fried elephant fish in Mekong style or the seared tuna with mint on a pomelo sauce or duck leg confit on a passion fruit sauce. The hot chocolate cake is a treat.

🍴🍴-🍴 Sao Hom, Nha Long Cho Co, T710-381 5616, http://saohom.transmekong.com. This new and very busy restaurant on the riverfront serves plentiful food and provides very good service. Watching the river life and the floating pleasure palaces at night is a good way to spend an evening meal here. Shame about the illuminated billboards on the opposite bank. This place is popular with large tour groups that alter the character of the restaurant when they swarm in.

🍴 Coffee-Bar New, 1 Ngo Quyen St. The latest youth hangout serving up coffee, food and loud music. The perfect people-watching spot opposite the old market area.

🍴 Hop Pho, 4-6 Ngo Gia Tu, T710-381 5208,

Open from 0630. New kid on the block, **Hop Pho** is all grey and black lines under umbrellas amid water features. It's a stylish hangout with abundant Vietnamese food. Try the avocado and durian ice cream.

🍴 Mekong, 38 Hai Ba Trung St. Perfectly good little place near the river in this popular restaurant strip. Serves decent Vietnamese fare at reasonable prices.

🍴 Nam Bo, 50 Hai Ba Trung St, T710-382 3908. Excellent little place serving tasty Vietnamese and French dishes in an attractive French house on the corner of the street; try to get a table on the balcony. The set menu is 170,000d. Small café downstairs.

🍴 Ninh Kieu, 2 Hai Ba Trung St. Part of the hotel complex. On the river, good seafood and some Western dishes. Popular local venue for wedding parties.

🍴 Phuong Nam, 48 Hai Ba Trung St, T71-812077. Similar to the nextdoor **Nam Bo**, good food, less stylish, a popular travellers' haunt and reasonable prices.

🍴 Thanh Thuy, No 149, 30 Thang 4, T710-384 0207. A popular goat hotpot restaurant run by a French Canadian and his Vietnamese wife. Goat, in Vietnam, particularly stewed testicles or testicle rice wine, is popular with men who believe that a good helping will boost their sexual potency. Any mention of goat normally results in giggles.

Soc Trang *p87*
Soc Trang has no outstanding eateries, but several restaurants on **Hai Ba Trung St** do simple and cheap rice dishes. **Khanh Hung Hotel** offers a range of good food. **Phong Lan Hotel** has some Western dishes on a largely Vietnamese menu.

Bac Lieu *p88*
Bac Lieu hotel, see page 93, has reasonable restaurants for breakfast, lunch and dinner.

🍴 Cong Tu Bac Lieu. This compound is popular all day. Serves up Vietnamese food in the surrounds of a colonial mansion.

🍴 Hai Ho, 103/4 Highway 1A, Ward 7, T781-

395 2026. Open for breakfast, lunch and dinner. A clean restaurant with a reasonable selection of Western and Vietnamese dishes. The service is friendly although staff don't understand any English.

Ca Mau p89

There are also plenty of very cheap restaurants close to the market on Ly Bon St.

† **Hu Tieu Nam Vang**, 2C Tran Hung Dao St, diagonally opposite **Hoang Gia** hotel. Cheap and friendly and serving hu tieu.

† **Sao Mai Cafe in the Sao Mai Hotel**, a few doors down from Trieu Phat. Serves *banh mi, bo* and *pho bo*.

† **Trieu Phat**, 26 Phan Ngoc Hien St. Serves *com* and *hu tieu*.

🍸 Bars and clubs

Can Tho p85, map p86

The **Golf Can Tho Hotel** and **Victoria Can Tho Hotel** have well-stocked bars (see Sleeping, above). The latest draw for young locals is **Coffee-Bar New** in the centre of town. It's got karaoke too and stays open until 0100.

⊛ Festivals and events

Soc Trang p87

For details of the **Oc Om Boc festival**, see page 87.

Bac Lieu p88

The main festival is the **Ngo boat racing** held at the same time as the Soc Trang Om Boc festival (see above and page 87) but it is overlooked in favour of the Soc Trang festival. If you wish to see the races in a more relaxed atmosphere then visit Bac Lieu.

⊙ Shopping

Can Tho p85, map p86

Coop Mart, corner of Ngo Quyen and Hoa Binh Sts. Open 0800-2200 and stocked with hundreds of items. Useful for picnics.

Phat Hanh Sach, 29 Phan Dinh St. A

bookshop which also sells local maps.

Soc Trang p87

Soc Trang is renowned for the beautiful, locally made gold statues; a bargain for the quality on offer.

⛰ Activities and tours

Can Tho p85, map p86
Boat trips

Trans Mekong, 97/10 Ngo Quyen, P An Cu, T710-382 9540, www.transmekong. com. Operates the *Bassac*, a converted 24-m wooden rice barge that can sleep 12 passengers in 6 a/c cabins with private bathrooms. Prices include dinner and breakfast, entry tickets to visited sites, a French- or English-speaking guide on board and access to a small boat, *Bassac II*, catering for 24 guests. The **Victoria Can Tho** operates the *Lady Hau*, an upmarket converted rice barge for trips to the floating markets, US$50 per person (minimum 4 people). **Can Tho Tourist** operate trips.

Cookery classes

The **Victoria Can Tho** (see Sleeping, above) offers a Vietnamese cooking class in the hotel, in a rice field, at the 'Ancient House' or on its boat the *Lady Hau* with a trip to the local market from US$38 (minimum 2 people).

Swimming

The **Victoria Can Tho** (see Sleeping, above) has a pool open to the public for US$6.

Tennis

Tennis courts are available at the **Golf Hotel** and **Victoria Can Tho** (see Sleeping, above).

Therapies

The **Victoria Can Tho** boasts several massage cabins on the riverfront offering a host of treatments. Open to non-guests.

Tour operators

Can Tho Tourist, 20 Hai Ba Trung St, T710-

382 1852, http://canthotourist.vn. It's quite expensive and organizes tours in small boats and powerful boats – the latter not the best way to see the delta. The staff are helpful and knowledgeable. Tours include trips to Cai Rang, Phong Dien and Phung Hiep floating markets, to Soc Trang, city tours (328,000d), canal tours, bicycle tours, trekking tours, stork sanctuary tour and homestays that involve working with farmers in the fields. General boat tours also arranged. It charges US$60 for a 1 night tour for 2 including floating market and bike tour.

Victoria Can Tho, T710-381 0111, www.victoriahotels.asia. Expensive tours to see delta sights; city tour; floating markets and Soc Trang offered. The *Lady Hau* cruises to Cai Rang floating market (breakfast on board). Sunset cruises also possible.

Soc Trang *p87*
Tour operators
See **Soc Trang Tourist**, page 88.

Bac Lieu *p88*
Tour operators
 See **Bac Lieu Tourist Company**, page 89

Ca Mau *p89*
The main activities are botanical and bird-watching trips to U Minh Forest and the Mui Ca Mau National Park.

Tour operators
See **Minh Hai Tourist**, page 89.

⊖ Transport

Can Tho *p85, map p86*
Air
Vietnam Airlines, 66 Chau Van Liem St. The airport is situated about 7 km from the city centre. Flights to **Hanoi**. A taxi from the airport is 40,000-50,000d.

Bicycle
Bikes can be hired for US$4 a day from **Can Tho Tourist**, see Tour operators, above.

Boat
A bridge has been built to Can Tho but ferries will still operate for direct routing as the bridge is 10 km from Can Tho. There are no public boats leaving Can Tho.

Bus
The bus station is about 2 km northwest of town along Nguyen Trai St, at the intersection with Hung Vuong St. *Xe-ôm* is 10,000d into town. Hourly connections to **HCMC**'s Mien Tay terminal, 4-5 hrs, 80,000d (**Phuong Trang** bus company, T710-376 9768, provides a good service), and other towns in the Mekong Delta: **Rach Gia**, 0400-1800, 5 hrs, 60,000d; **Chau Doc**, 8 daily, 4 hrs, 55,000d; **Long Xuyen**, 6 daily, 33,000d; **My Tho**, hourly, 55,000d; **Vinh Long**, hourly, 55,000d; **Ca Mau**, hourly, 65,000d; **Soc Trang**, 35,000d. Can Tho Tourist, see Tour operators above, will book a ticket for you for 10,000d and includes transfer from your hotel to the bus station.

Cars
Cars with drivers can be hired from larger hotels.

Taxi
Mai Linh Taxi, T710-382 8282.

Soc Trang *p87*
Bus
Buses to **Ca Mau**, **Can Tho**, **Rach Gia** and **HCMC**.

Motorbike
Soc Trang is normally reached on Highway 1 from **Can Tho** but it's possible to get here from **Tra Vinh** by a single ferry crossing (there are several per hr) but note it's not a car ferry.

Bac Lieu *p88*
Bus
Buses go to **Soc Trang**, **Can Tho**, HCMC, **Ca Mau** and **Long Xuyen** from the station on Hai Ba Trung St

Ca Mau *p89*
Air
The airport is located at 93 Ly Thuong Kiet St heading out of town. Flights to **HCMC**.

Boat
It is possible to take a daily ferry (3 times a day) from Ca Mau to **Rach Gia**, from Ferry Pier B (located off Cao Thang St near the floating market), 100,000d.

Travelling by road up to Rach Gia, there is a river crossing, the Tac Cau Ferry (20,000d, moto 10,000d) after which there is a brand new road up to Rach Gia.

Bus
Ca Mau is almost at the end of Highway 1A. Bac Lieu, Soc Trang and onwards connection to Can Tho are along Highway 1A. Rach Gia is reached by Highway 63. Good bus connections to **Can Tho**, **Bac Lieu**, **Soc Trang** and **Rach Gia**. The bus service to **HCMC** takes 11 hrs by regular bus and 8 hrs by express, daily 0530-1030.

❶ Directory

Can Tho *p85, map p86*
Banks These are all the way along Phan Dinh Phung St. **BIDV**, 29-31 Chau Van Liem St. Visa and MasterCard ATM. **Vietinbank**, 9 Phan Dinh Phung St, at the corner with Ngo Quyen. Changes TCs, Visa ATM. **Agriank**, 3 Phan Dinh Phung St. **Sacombank**, 99 Vo Van Tan St. Visa and MasterCard ATM. **Vietcombank**, 7 Hoa Binh Blvd, T710-382 0445. Bureau de change service. **Hospitals** 4 Chau Van Liem St, T710-382 0071. **Internet** Pizza_CT, 9 Chau Van Liem St. Alternatively, the big hotels (see Sleeping, above) have email facilities. **Post office** 2 Hoa Binh Blvd, T710-382 7280.

Soc Trang *p87*
Banks Vietcombank, 27 Hai Ba Trung St. **Hospitals** 15 Pasteur St, T79-382 5201. **Internet** Available in the post office. 0700-2000. **Post office** 2 Tran Hung Dao St.

Bac Lieu *p88*
Banks BIDV, Lo 42-44, Hoa Binh Blvd, Ward 3. **Hospitals** 128 Nguyen Hue St, Ward 3, T781-382 2297. **Internet** At the post office. **Post office** Tran Phu St, Ward 3.

Ca Mau *p89*
Banks Incombank, Hung Vuong St, opposite the main post office. Bureau de change, credit card cash advances. **Hospitals** Ca Mau Hospital, Phan Anh Dao St, Khom 1, T780-383 1015. **Internet** The main post office is the best place. **Post office** 3 Luu Tan Tai St, Ward 5.

Chau Doc and around

Chau Doc was once an attractive bustling riverside town (formerly called Chau Phu) in An Giang Province on the west bank of the Hau or Bassac River and bordering Cambodia. It is still a bustling market town but no longer so appealing. The town is an important trading and marketing centre for the surrounding agricultural communities. One of its biggest attractions is the nearby Nui Sam (Sam Mountain), which is dotted with pagodas and tombs and from whose summit superb views of the plains below can be enjoyed. Around Chau Doc are the towns of Rach Gia, Ha Tien and, capital of the province, Long Xuyen. ▸▸ *For listings, see pages 104-110.*

Ins and outs

Getting there Chau Doc is an increasingly important border crossing into Cambodia. There are connections by boat with Phnom Penh as well as by road. It is also possible (but expensive) to get to Chau Doc by boat from Can Tho (private charter only or by the Victoria Hotel group boat for guests only). Road connections with Can Tho, Vinh Long and Ho Chi Minh City are good. ▸▸ *See Transport, page 108.*

Getting around Chau Doc itself is easily small enough to explore on foot. By means of a bridge or sampan crossing, some nearby Cham villages can be reached and explored on foot too. Nui Sam, the nearby sacred mountain, can be reached by motorbike or bus.

Best time to visit Chau Doc suffers not only from the universal Mekong problem of the monsoon floods, but also from the fact that Nui Sam is one of the holiest sites in southern Vietnam and, as such, attracts vast numbers of pilgrims on auspicious days. From a climatic viewpoint then the best time to visit is December to April.

Tourist information Tour operators in town are a good source of information. ▸▸ *See Tour operators page 108.*

History

Until the mid-18th century Chau Doc was part of Cambodia: it was given to the Nguyen lord, Nguyen Phuc Khoat, after he had helped to put down a local insurrection. The area still supports a large Khmer population, as well as the largest Cham settlement in the Delta. Cambodia's influence can be seen in the tendency for women to wear the *kramar*, Cambodia's famous chequered scarf, instead of the *non lá* conical hat, and in the people's darker skin, indicating Khmer blood. Chau Doc district (it was a separate province for a while) is the seat of the **Hoa Hao religion**, which claims about one to 1.5 million adherents and was founded in the village of Hoa Hao in 1939 (see page 100).

Chau Doc → *For listings, see pages 104-110.*

A large market sprawls from the riverfront down and along Le Cong Thanh Doc, Phu Thu, Bach Dang and Chi Lang streets. It sells fresh produce and black-market goods smuggled across from Cambodia. Near the market and the river, at the intersection of Tran Hung Dao Street and Nguyen Van Thoai Street, is the **Chau Phu Pagoda**. Built in 1926, it is dedicated to Thai Ngoc Hau, a former local mandarin. The pagoda is rather dilapidated, but has some fine carved pillars, which miraculously are still standing. A **Cao Dai temple**, which welcomes visitors, stands on Louise Street.

The **Vinh Te Canal**, north of town, is 90 km long and is a considerable feat of engineering, begun in 1819 and finished in 1824 using 80,000 workers. Its purpose was twofold: navigation and defence from the Cambodians. So impressed was Emperor Minh Mang in the achievement of its builder, Nguyen Van Thoai (or Thoai Ngoc Hau), that he named the canal after Thoai's wife, Chau Thi Vinh Te.

Around Chau Doc → *For listings, see pages 104-110.*

Easily visited from Chau Doc is the holy mountain, Nui Sam, covered in pagodas. Across the river you can boat over to Cham villages and see the floating fish farms. South of Chau Doc the road passes the sorrowful Ba Chuc ossuary. There are also three international border crossings to Cambodia, two to the southwest and one to the north of Chau Doc.

Nui Sam (Sam Mountain)
ⓘ *Take a bus (there is a stop at the foot of the mountain) or xe lôi.*
Nui Sam lies about 5 km southwest of town and is one reason to visit Chau Doc. This mountain was designated a 'Famed Beauty Spot' in 1980 by the Ministry of Culture. It

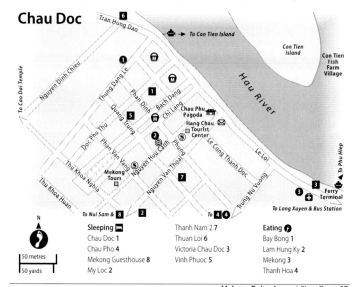

Chau Doc

Sleeping 🛏
Chau Doc 1
Chau Pho 1
Mekong Guesthouse 8
My Loc 2
Thanh Nam 2 7
Thuan Loi 6
Victoria Chau Doc 3
Vinh Phuoc 5

Eating 🍴
Bay Bong 1
Lam Hung Ky 2
Mekong 3
Thanh Hoa 4

is one of the holiest sites in southern Vietnam. Rising from the flood plain, Nui Sam is a favourite spot for Vietnamese tourists who throng here, especially at festival time.

The mountain, really a barren, rock-strewn hill, can be seen at the end of the continuation of Nguyen Van Thoai Street. It is literally honeycombed with tombs, sanctuaries and temples. Most visitors come only to see Tay An Pagoda, Lady Xu Temple, and the tomb of Thoai Ngoc Hau (see above). But it is possible to walk or drive right up the hill for good views of the surrounding countryside: from the summit it is easy to appreciate that this is some of the most fertile land in Vietnam. At the top is a military base formerly occupied by American soldiers and now by Vietnamese watching their Cambodian flank. Near the top the **Victoria Hotel** group has built a hotel used for conferences only.

The **Tay An Pagoda** is at the foot of the hill, facing the road. Built originally in 1847, it has been extended twice and now represents an eclectic mixture of styles – Chinese, Islamic, perhaps even Italian. The pagoda contains a bewildering display of more than 200 statues. A short distance on from the pagoda, to the right, past shops and stalls, is the **Chua Xu**. This temple was originally constructed in the late 19th century, and then rebuilt in 1972. It is rather a featureless building, though highly revered by the Vietnamese and honours the holy Lady Xu whose statue is enshrined in the new multi-roofed pagoda. The 23rd to the 25th of the fourth lunar month is the period when the holy Lady is commemorated, during which time, hundreds of Vietnamese flock to see her being washed and reclothed. Lady Xu is a major pilgrimage for traders and business from Ho Chi Minh City and the south, all hoping that sales will thereby soar and profits leap. On the other side of the road is the **tomb of Thoai Ngoc Hau** (1761-1829); an enormous head of the man graces the entranceway. Thoai is a local hero having played a role in the resistance against the French but more for his engineering feats in canal building and draining swamps. He is also known as Nguyen Van Thoai and this name is given to one of Chau Doc's streets. The real reason to come here is to watch the pilgrims and to climb the hill.

Hang Pagoda, a 200-year-old temple situated halfway up Nui Sam, is worth visiting for several reasons. In the first level of the temple are some vivid cartoon drawings of the tortures of hell. The second level is built at the mouth of a cave which last century was home to a woman named Thich Gieu Thien. Her likeness and tomb can be seen in the first pagoda. Fed up with her lazy and abusive husband she left her home in Cholon and came to live in this cave, as an ascetic supposedly waited on by two snakes.

Nui Sam is the most expensive burial site in southern Vietnam. Wealthy Vietnamese and Chinese believe it is a most propitious last resting place. This is why the lower flanks are given over almost entirely to tombs. Demand for burial plots has reached such levels that a new complex is being developed to help ease the demands on the land at Sam Mountain.

Cham villages

There are a number of Cham villages around Chau Doc. **Phu Hiep**, **Con Tien** and **Chau Giang** are on the opposite bank of the Hau River. There are several mosques in the villages as the Cham in this part of Vietnam are Muslim. At **Chau Phong** visitors can enjoy homestays. To reach the villages, take a sampan from the ferry terminal near the **Victoria Chau Doc Hotel**.

A visit to the **floating fish farm villages** (some 3000 floating houses), such as **Con Tien**, is a worthwhile and informative experience. A floating farm will have some 150,000 carp contained in a 6-m-deep iron cage beneath the house. Fish are worth around 600d for a baby and up to 25,000d for 500 g for a five-month-old fish. Catfish and mullet are also raised. (Chau Doc has a catfish monument on the riverfront promenade). When the fish are ready for sale, boats with nets under them are used to transport the fish to Long Xuyen.

Border crossings to Cambodia

It is possible to cross the border to Cambodia north of Chau Doc at the **Vinh Xuong** (Omsano in Cambodia) boat crossing; just south of Chau Doc at **Tinh Bien** near Nha Ban (Phnom Den, Takeo, on the Cambodian side), and at **Xà Xía**, near Ha Tien (Prek Chak in Cambodia). It is possible to exit at Vinh Xuong and get a Cambodian visa but it's not possible to get a Vietnamese visa to enter Vietnam. At Tinh Bien you can buy a Cambodian visa but not a Vietnamese visa on entering. (*Xe ôm* to Tinh Bien from Chau Doc, US$6; private transfer, US$40.) At Xà Xía, you can get a Cambodian visa for US$25 but not a Vietnamese visa. There is a Vietnam consulate in Sihanoukville.

Chau Doc to Ha Tien

Ha Tien can be reached either by boat or by road. The road is in a pitiful state but can be traversed by 4WD, Minsk or bicycle. Nevertheless, it is well worth attempting as it means the south coast can be reached without trailing back the 38 km to Long Xuyen. Also, the scenery as the road skirts the Cambodian border is beautiful and the local way of life little changed in hundreds of years. The road passes **Ba Chuc ossuary** where the bones of 1000 Vietnamese killed in 1978 by the Khmer Rouge are displayed in a glass-sided memorial. Skulls are also stacked up in a glass-sided memorial, and each section is categorized by gender and by age – from children to grandparents. Nearby, there is a house in a small row of shops where photographs of the massacre are displayed; they are grisly and abhorrent.

An alternative route to Ha Tien is to follow Highway 91 to Nha Ban town. Turn right and follow the signs to Tri Ton town (along the way you drive through the Plain of Reeds, pass Cam Mountain and also various Khmer temples that are beautiful and thankfully tourist free. Upon arrival in Tri Ton town (some of the shops have signs in Khmer script) turn right and head for the Vam Ray ferry. Once across the Ha Tien-Rach Gia canal you are on Highway 80. Turn left to Rach Gia and right to Ha Tien.

Long Xuyen → *For listings, see pages 104-110.*

Sprawling for miles along the west bank of the Bassac or Hau River is Long Xuyen, capital of An Giang Province. Driving along the dazzling new dual carriageways into town one anticipates something rather splendid but Long Xuyen disappoints for there is nothing of any interest at the end. It is rather surprising that such a large town can so spectacularly fail to produce anything of real note. The town is not mired in poverty but agreeably well off. In fact there is an attractive sense of civic pride and this is demonstrated in the 'cared for' feel of the place and in its new university which is notable for its well-regarded faculty of agriculture.

Rice fields predominate and small villages huddle under the shade of fruit trees. The architecture is traditional and modest in scale: houses retain their pitched tile roofs and incorporate plenty of wood. The region remains isolated, for the time being, from the demands of the 21st century, so life proceeds at the pace its people have been familiar with for a hundred years. The roads are narrow, traffic is light and for visitors with time to spare a tour by bicycle or on motorbike is easily the best way to see the area.

Ins and outs

Getting there and around The quickest way is direct from Ho Chi Minh City with one ferry crossing at Long Xuyen itself. There are plenty of taxis, an efficient local bus service and a plethora of *Honda ôm* drivers. ▶▶ *See Transport, page 108.*

Tourist information An Giang Tourimex ① *80 Tran Hung Dao St, T76-384 1036, http://www.angiangtourimex.com/aboutus.htm.*

History
Long Xuyen was once the main centre for the Hoa Hao religious sect. They believed in simplicity and as such built no structures. Up until 1956 they had their own militia and were, along with the Cao Dai sect, a major military force in the south. Long Xuyen has two main claims to fame. Firstly, nearby Ong Ho Island was the birthplace of Ton Duc Thang, who, when he worked in the Bason Shipyard in Saigon, agitated against the French. As a result he served a term on Con Dao Island. In 1946 he went to Hanoi and became friends with Ho Chi Minh. Upon the latter's death in 1969 Ton Duc Thang became president of North Vietnam and, in 1975, was the first president of united Vietnam.

Sights
The large **Roman Catholic Cathedral** ① *Hung Vuong St*, is visible from out of town; two clasped hands form the spire. It was completed shortly before reunification in 1975.

A short walk away is **Quan Thanh Pagoda** ① *8 Le Minh Nguyen St*, which contains lively murals on the entrance wall and the figure of General Quan Cong and his two mandarin companions General Chau Xuong and Mandarin Quan Binh at the altar. Also on Le Minh Nguyen Street, close to the intersection with Huynh Thi Huong Street, is the **Dinh Than My Phuoc Pagoda**. Note the roof and the murals on the wooden walls near the altar.

An Giang Museum ① *77 Thoai Ngoc Hau St, T76-384 1251, 0730-1030, 1400-1630*, is a pleasant enough museum. Primarily geared to the life and times of Ton Duc Thang it also houses relics from Oc-Eo but probably of more interest is a display showing the changing ways of life from the 1930s until the present day .

On the outskirts of town on Tran Hung Dao Street travelling towards Chau Doc (just after the second bridge, about 500 m), the **Cao Dai church** is worth visiting, especially if you are unable to see the Cao Dai temple at Tay Ninh.

Ong Ho Island is a pleasant trip up the Hau River for fans of Bac Ton (Uncle Ton). Boats leave from the riverfront.

Rach Gia → *For listings, see pages 104-110.*

Rach Gia has undergone somewhat of a transformation in recent years. It has gone from being a rather unpleasant little town to a thriving port with a new urban development on reclaimed land at Lan Bien on the coast south of the city. Already an entry point for goods, both smuggled and legal, from Thailand, the port has grown in significance as trade with neighbouring ASEAN countries has developed. The centre of the town is in fact an island at the mouth of the Cai Lon River. There are a number of pagodas to visit. The wharf area is interesting and the bustling fish market displays the wealth of the seas here. Some attractive colonial architecture survives.

Rach Gia is the capital of Kien Giang Province. The wealth of the province is based on rice, seafood and trade. *Nuoc mam*, the renowned Vietnamese fish sauce, is also produced here.

Ins and outs
Getting there There are daily flights from Ho Chi Minh City and Phu Quoc. In the peak season it is advisable to book well in advance as the flights tend to fill up fast. There are good road connections with Ha Tien, Long Xuyen, Can Tho. There are also boats to Phu Quoc.

Tourist information Kien Giang Travel Co ① *5 Le Loi St, T77-386 7687, nguyendaihokg@ gmail.com*, is the government tourist office and is helpful and friendly but little English is spoken. See also Tour operators for other sources of information.

History

As the straight blue lines on any good map will show, several highly impressive canals converge on Rach Gia. Nguyen Van Thoai, builder of the Chau Doc to Ha Tien canal, built the straight-as-an-arrow Long Xuyen to Rach Gia canal in 1822. Highway 80, along which most visitors drive to Rach Gia, runs alongside the canal. It was formerly named the Thoai canal in honour of its builder but maps today simply call it the Cai San canal. The O Mon canal was built by the French in 1896 and in 1955 the Rach Soi–Kien Luong canal was built to transport clinker from Kien Luong plant to the Thu Duc cement works on the outskirts of Saigon.

Sights

Rach Gia's pagodas include the **Phat Lon Pagoda**, which is on the mainland north of town just off Quang Trung Street, and the **Nguyen Trung Truc Temple**, which is not far away at 18 Nguyen Cong Tru Street, close to the port. The latter is dedicated to the 19th-century Vietnamese resistance leader of the same name. Nguyen Trung Truc was active in Cochin China during the 1860s, and led the raid that resulted in the attack on the French warship *Esperance*. As the French closed in, he retreated to the island of Phu Quoc. From here, the French only managed to dislodge him after threatening to kill his mother. He gave himself up and was executed at the market place in Rach Gia on 27 October 1868. His statue also dominates the main small city park at the top of Le Loi street and the riverbank.

   Tam Bao Temple dates from the 18th century but was rebuilt in 1917. During the First Indochina War it was used to conceal Viet Minh nationalists who published a newspaper from here. There is the small **Rach Gia Museum** ① *27 Nguyen Van Troi St, T77-386 3727, Mon-Fri 0700-1100, free*, which houses a good selection of pottery and artefacts from Oc-Eo in a lovely old building. It was undergoing repairs at the time of publication.

Oc-Eo

① *The site is near the village of Tan Hoi and is only accessible by boat. Hire a small boat (the approach canal is very shallow and narrow) from the river front beyond the Vinh Tan Van Market, northeast along Bach Dang St. The trip takes several hours. Entrance 60,000d*
Oc-Eo is an ancient city about 10 km inland from Rach Gia. It is of great interest and significance to archaeologists, but there is not a great deal for the visitor to see bar a pile of stones on which sits a small bamboo shrine. The site is overseen by an elderly custodian who lives adjacent to it. This port city of the ancient kingdom of Funan (see page 101) was at its height between the first and sixth centuries AD. Excavations have shown that buildings were constructed on piles and the city was interlinked by a complex network of irrigation and transport canals. Like many of the ancient empires of the region, Oc-Eo built its wealth on controlling trade between the East (China) and the West (India and the Mediterranean). Vessels from Malaya, Indonesia and Persia docked here. No sculpture has yet been found, but a gold medallion with the profile of the Roman emperor Antonius Pius (AD 152) has been unearthed

Ha Tien used to be a quaint small town with a tranquil pace of life and an attractive US-built pontoon bridge that carried bikers and pedestrians across to the opposite bank of the river. It has quite rapidly become a sprawling urban mess with ugly hotels cluttering the riverbank and construction running rampant with no regard to aesthetic. The boom has no doubt been helped by the opening of the border with Cambodia at Xà Xía. Step back off the main thoroughfare and you will find vestiges of the quaint appeal that once made this city worth visiting. After the drive from either Chau Doc or Rach Gia a drink on the stilted **café** is a relaxing way to pass the afternoon.

Ins and outs

Getting there Ha Tien can be reached by road from Chau Doc, Rach Gia and also by ferry from Phu Quoc Island. The first 20 km before Ha Tien on Highway 80 and the first 10 km out of Rach Gia are interesting. The rest of the journey is monotonous. It can also be reached by crossing the border from Cambodia at Xà Xía. See border crossings with Cambodia, page 99. In the town itself there are one or two taxis and plenty of *Honda ôm* drivers.

Tourist information Ha Tien Tourism Coop Ltd ⓘ *1 Phuong Thanh St, T77-395 9598, hatientourism@gmail.com*. Run by the helpful Marie, this new private tourism service is a great boon for tourists, especially those coming in from Cambodia. Boat and bus tickets and free internet for guests. There's also food.

History

Ha Tien's history is strongly coloured by its proximity to Cambodia, to which the area belonged until the 18th century. The numerical and agricultural superiority of the Vietnamese allowed them to gradually displace the Khmer occupants and eventually military might, under Mac Cuu, prevailed. But it is not an argument the Khmer are prepared to walk away from, as their incursions into the area in the late 1970s showed, and bitter resentments remain on both sides of the border. Unfortunately, the floating pontoon built by US army engineers was dismantled a few years ago.

Sights

Despite its colourful history, modern Ha Tien does not contain a great deal of interest to the visitor and apart from a handful of buildings there is little of architectural merit.

There are a number of pagodas in town. The **Tam Bao Temple**, at 328 Phuong Thanh Street, was founded in the 18th century, as too was **Chua Phu Dung (Phu Dung Pagoda)** which can be found a short distance along a path to the northwest just off Phuong Thanh Street. A lengthy story is attached to this temple, the 'Cotton Rose Hibiscus Pagoda'. In 1730, newly widowed Nguyen Nghi fled invaders from Laos and landed in Ha Tien with his son and 10-year-old daughter, Phu Cu (the ancient form of Phu Dung with the same floral meaning). Nguyen Nghi was soon appointed Professor of Literature and Poetry to Duke Mac Cuu's son, Mac Tu (see Den Mac Cuu, below) and privately tutored his own little daughter, who had taken to dressing as a boy in order to be able to attend school. After Duke Mac Cuu's untimely death in 1735 his son was granted the name Mac Thien Tich and the title Great Admiral Commander-in-Chief, Plenipotentiary Minister of Ha Tien Province. Later he inaugurated a poetry club at which young Phu Cu, still in the guise of a boy, declaimed exquisitely, setting passions ablaze. Surreptitious investigations put the Great Admiral's mind at rest: 'he' was in fact a girl. A long poetic romance and royal wedding followed.

After years of happy marriage the angelic Phu Cu one day begged her husband to let her break with their poetic love of the past and become a nun. The Great Admiral realized he could not but comply. He built the Phu Cu, Cotton Rose Hibiscus Pagoda, wherein his beloved wife spent the rest of her life in prayer and contemplation. The towering pagoda was built so high that it served as a constant reminder and could, in due course, be seen from his own tomb.

Den Mac Cuu, the temple dedicated to the worship of the Mac Cuu and his clan, was built in 1898-1902. Mac Cuu was provincial governor under the waning Khmer rule and in

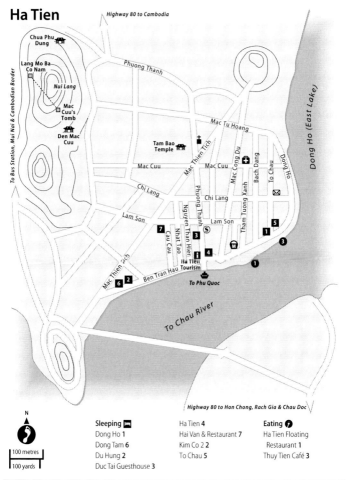

Ha Tien

Sleeping 🛏	Ha Tien **4**	Eating 🍴
Dong Ho **1**	Hai Van & Restaurant **7**	Ha Tien Floating
Dong Tam **6**	Kim Co 2 **2**	Restaurant **1**
Du Hung **2**	To Chau **5**	Thuy Tien Café **3**
Duc Tai Guesthouse **3**		

1708 established a Vietnamese protectorate. The temple lies a short way from the town and sits at the foot of Nui Lang (Tomb Mountain). To the left of the altar house is a map showing the location of the tombs of members of the clan. Mac Cuu's own tomb lies a short distance up the hill along a path leading from the right of the temple, from where there are good views of the sea.

Around the back of Nui Lang (a short drive, or longish trek) is **Lang Mo Ba Co Nam** (tomb of Great Aunt Number Five), an honorary title given to the three-year-old daughter of Mac Cuu who was buried alive. It has become an important shrine to Vietnamese seeking her divine intercession in time of family crisis and is more visited than Mac Cuu's tomb.

Around Ha Tien

Mui Nai ① *small entrance fee*, lies in a 'tourist park' about 5 km west of town. There are some nicely wooded hills and a muddy beach from where Phu Quoc Island and Cambodia can be seen. The beach gets very crowded and litter-strewn during public holidays. It offers the opportunity of rock scrambling for the nimble-footed but is disappointing compared with the sandy beach at Hon Chong.

Thach Dong Pagoda ① *5000d*, 3 km from Ha Tien, and a short hike up from the road, is dedicated to the goddess Quan Am; at the bottom of the mountain is **Bia Cam Thu** (Monument of Hate; the Vietnamese don't mince their words) a memorial to the 130 Vietnamese slain by the Khmer Rouge in March 1978. The temple is inside a limestone hill that consists of a series of caves and clefts in the rock. There are good views of the surrounding, remarkably flat, country. About 2 km beyond Thach Dong Pagoda is the **Cambodian border** at Xà Xía, see page 99.

Hon Chong is a popular and well known beach area about 30 km east of Ha Tien. Unlike Ha Tien, Hon Chong has miles of beach which can get dirty and littered although it is much nicer than Ha Tien but not a patch on Phu Quoc. The beach area is undeveloped apart from a string of cafés set back behind the casuarina trees with chairs and hammocks where you can sup a beer. Apart from the beach its main claim to fame is the **holy grotto** and the interesting limestone formations **Hon Phu Tu** (Father and Son rocks), which lie 100 m or so offshore. To get to Hon Chong by car, turn south off Highway 80 at Kien Luong, 18 km, or take a bus to Kien Luong, or *xe ôm* to Hon Chong (130,000d, 20 minutes); it's very dusty. Once in Hon Chong, boats are available to the grotto and to Ngo Island.

Follow the path through **Chua Hang** (Hang Pagoda), to the beach. The temple with its Buddha of 100 hands loses much of its religious significance and atmosphere at holiday times (notably Tet) when noisy throngs of trippers file through on their way to the beach.

Chau Doc and around listings

For Sleeping and Eating price codes and other relevant information, see pages 10-13.

☐ Sleeping

Chau Doc *p97, map p97*
$$$$ Victoria Chau Doc, 32 Le Loi St, T76-386 5010, www.victoriahotels-asia.com. The old building was entirely renovated by this excellent French hotel group, to produce a lovely hotel right on the river. It is comfortable, equipped with a pool and all mod cons. Its outdoor terrace is the perfect place to drink and watch the hustle and bustle on the Mekong. The hotel group runs a speedboat to and from Phnom Penh.
$$ Chau Pho, Trung Nu Vuong St, Ward B, T76-356 4139, www.chauphohotel.com.

This 38-room hotel is very comfortable and quiet but the occasional lack of hot water shouldn't happen at these prices; it's a 10-min walk from the town centre. Breakfast is included and has improved. Wi-fi available.

$ Delta Floating Hotel, 443 Le Loi St (Casu Lo Heo), Phu Hiep Ward, next to the Chau Doc Tourist Pier, T76-355 0838.These 10 rooms on the water are small and airless and overpriced but some have balconies and they feature mosquito nets. There's a café and restaurant on the adjacent floating boats and it would be a novel way to spend the night in Chau Doc but note that river traffic starts very early on the Mekong.

$ Ngoc Phu (formerly **Chau Doc**), 17 Doc Phu Thu St, T76-386 6484. The staff are friendly although very little English is spoken. The rooms (a/c or fan) are large, clean and equipped with basic facilities.

$ Thuan Loi, 18 Tran Hung Dao St, T76-386 6134, hotelthuanloi@hcm.vnn.vn. A/c and good river views, clean and friendly. The expanded and attractively designed restaurant enjoys a great location right on the river and is recommended especially in the late afternoon for coffee. This is a highly popular place; reserve in advance if possible.

$ Thanh Nam 2, 10 Quang Trung St, T76-321 2616, thanhnam2hotel@yahoo.com. Rooms are nicer here than the **Vinh Phuoc** if you can stand the bright green floor tiles. There are 10 rooms; those with a/c are slightly more expensive.

$ Vinh Phuoc, 12-14 Quang Trung St, T76-356 3013, vinhphuochotel@yahoo.com. A/c rooms are slightly more expensive than fan rooms.

Nui Sam *p97*

Almost every café near Sam Mountain has a room for rent and you can get good value by shopping around and bargaining hard.

$$ Ben Da Sam Mountain Resort, Highway 91, T76-386 1745. This resort consists of 4 hotels, a restaurant and bar. The staff speak good English. If you want a little bit of luxury then this would be the place to stay. Sam Mountain is 5 mins' walk away.

Cham villages *p98*

$ Cham Communities Based Tourism Village, T76-395 2541, sodulichangiang@vnn.vn. Contact **Ang Giang Tourism** to have the opportunity to stay in Chau Phong, a Cham village close to Chau Doc.

Long Xuyen *p99*

$$-$ Dong Xuyen Hotel, 9A Luong Van Cu St, T76-384 1365, longxuyenhotel@hcm.vnn.vn. The rooms all come equipped with a/c, en suite facilities, minibar. The hotel itself has massage, steam bath and jacuzzi. The staff speak good English and are helpful.

$$ Long Xuyen, 19 Nguyen Van Cung St, T76-384 1927, longxuyenhotel@hcm.vnn.vn. A/c, hot water, restaurant. Cheaper than the **Dong Xuyen** hotel. The staff are friendly and the rooms are adequate.

Rach Gia *p100*

$ Hoang Gia 2, 32 Le Thanh Ton St, T77-392 0980, www.hoanggiahotels.com.vn. Located near the bus station with smartly decorated rooms.

$ Hong Nam, Lo B1, Ly Thai To St, T77-387 3090, opposite the market area and convenient for the bus station. Rooms are comfortable but make sure you ask for a room on the interior; the ones facing the street suffer a bit from noise.

$ Kim Co, 141 Nguyen Hung Son St, T77-387 9610, www.kimcohotel.com. The pastel shades of this hotel are incongruous in the surrounding streets. Still, it's well located. Breakfast not included. Wi-fi available.

Ha Tien *p102, map p103*

$$-$ Ha Tien Hotel, 36 Tran Hau St, T77-385 1563. In a convenient location close to the ferry station with a nice alfresco restaurant. However, the 30 rooms are a little lacklustre despite it being a new hotel and are a tad overpriced; those with balconies cost more.

$ Dong Ho, 2 Tran Hau St, T77-385 2141. This yellow-shuttered building is on the quiet and quaint riverside of Ha Tien. Rooms are brighter and a little smarter than at neighbouring **To Chau** although they are basic. Those with a balcony overlooking the river and pontoon bridge are a must. All the rooms have twin beds, en suite bathrooms. Some a/c is available.

$ Dong Tam, 83 Tran Hau St, T77-395 0555, www.dongtamhotel.com. A less professional outfit than the sister hotel the **Du Hung**. Staff refuse to serve Vietnamese coffee because they think you won't like it; bizarre.

$ Du Hung, 27A Tran Hau St, T77-395 1555, www.dongtamhotel.com. A recommended hotel with spacious rooms and all facilities close to the ferry station.

$ Duc Tai Guesthouse, 9 Phuong Thanh St, T77-385 2405. At the end of the street is the main market for Ha Tien. If you are an early riser then this hotel would suit you well. Rooms are en suite and basically furnished with a/c or fans.

$ Hai Van, 55 Lam Son St, T77-385 2872. This new hotel with attached restaurant offers a comfortable rooms a few block backs from the hustle, bustle and building works on Tran Hau Street.

$ Kim Co 2, 21-23 Tran Hau St, T77-395 7957, www.kimcohotel.com. A good central option on the main strip.

$ To Chau, 56 Dong Ho St, T77-385 2148. A small hotel on the riverfront with views that commend it. Rooms are very large but also very spartan. They all come equipped with a/c, TV, minibar and en suite facilities with hot water. Try and opt for a room with a view of the To Chau River as it'll have a balcony. The owner and his family are friendly but they only speak a little English.

Hon Chong *p104*

$$$-$$ Hon Trem Resort, T77-385 4331, www.kiengiangtourist.com.vn. Built in the most fantastic location overlooking the bay at Hon Chong, it is rather under utilized. Rooms enjoy beautiful views that can be seen from the bed through the floor-to-ceiling windows. The massage centre is a little unloved but there's plans for a pool. Opt for a villa over the rooms in the ugly

block at the foot of the hill on which the resort is perched. There's no beach to access here which is disappointing. Bikes can be rented.

$$-$ Green Hill Guest House, 905 Hon Chong, Binh An, T77-385 4369. A friendly, clean and comfortable white guesthouse perched on a hill with excellent views of the bay from the spacious top bedrooms.

$ My Lan, opposite Duong Beach on the other side of the road, T77-375 9044, mylanhotel@vnn.vn. A secure, gated hotel with excellent-value large, clean rooms on the beach road. The rooms are in smart, new bungalows with TV, ceiling fan, a/c and shower units. The 24-hr restaurant does a good breakfast. The menu is not in English but some staff speak basic English..

Eating

Chau Doc *p97, map p97*

¶¶¶-¶¶ La Bassac, in Victoria Chau Doc, see Sleeping, above. The extravagant French and Vietnamese menus at this riverside restaurant outstrip the decor which has the air of a conservatory. Ignoring this, tuck into delicious meals of duck, rack of lamb or prawns. You won't be disappointed.

¶ Bay Bong, 22 Thung Dang Le St, T76-386 7271. Specializes in hot pots and soups and also offers a good choice of fresh fish. The staff are friendly.

¶ Lam Hung Ky, 71 Chi Lang St. Excellent freshly prepared and cooked food. There'sa wide range of food stalls in the market area.

¶ Mekong, 41 Le Loi St, T76-386 7381, opposite **Victoria Chau Doc**, open for lunch and dinner. It is located in a lovingly restored French villa. Good selection of food and the staff are friendly.

¶ Thanh Hoa, Trung Nu Vuong St. Choose from the dozens of shellfish aquariums and platters at this buzzing restaurant.

¶ Vinh Phuoc, see Sleeping, above. 0630-2230. Pretty standard Western and Vietnamese food with good, friendly service.

Long Xuyen *p99*

All the hotels have restaurants.

¶ Long Xuyen, corner of Nguyen Trai and Hai Ba Trung St. Good Chinese and Western food. Specializes in seafood.

Rach Gia *p100*

¶ Hai Au, 2 Nguyen Trung Truc St, T77-386 3740. Good choice of food, well presented with decent-sized portions in a smart building with a lovely outdoor terraced area covered in creepers overlooking the river.

¶ Sen Hong Hoan Hi, G20-21 Huynh Thuc Khang St, T77-325 4447, just around the corner from the bus station is a cosy and popular place, lit with fairy lights, to kick back with a coffee or fruit shake waiting for your departure.

¶ Valentine, 37 Hung Vuong St. Comfortable restaurant offering up plenty of sautéed dishes as well as omelettes and shellfish and steamed fish dishes.

¶ Vinh Hong 2, 194 Lam Quang Ky St, T77-387 7870. Preferred choice for the locals. Vietnamese fare only but well cooked, well and presented and cheap.

Cafés

There is a good selection on **Nguyen Trung Truc**, **Nguyen Thai Hoc** and **Tran Hung Dao** STs. **Cafe Yumi**, corner of Lac Hong and Pham Hung Sts, and **Cafe Ja**, corner of Le Van Huu and Bui Huy Bich Sts behind Citimart are 2 smart hangouts in the new district of Lan Bien on reclaimed land. These are the latest hangouts for young Vietnamese. At the centre of the coastal strip is the Lac Hong Park where you'll find stalls, cafés and the **Lagoon Seafood Center** as well as dozens of folk flying colourful kites.

Ha Tien *p102, map p103*

There are numerous food stalls along the river and **Ben Tran Hau** and **Dong Ho** streets.

¶¶-¶ Hai Van, 55 Lam Son St, T77-385 2872. This restaurant has moved from its popular riverside spot to be at the back end of a hotel of the same name and has smartened

up its appearance. It serves up a reasonable selection of Chinese, Vietnamese and international cuisine.

¶ Ha Tien Floating Restaurant, T77-395 9939. Quite a nice surprise for Ha Tien with Australian beef on the menu. There's a huge menu of chicken, frog and eel as well as fish. Popular with local businesspeople.

Cafés

Thanh Nam, Tran Hau St. Great smoothies and is a good for people-watching.

Thuy Tien Café, Nguyen Van Hai St. This is the pick of the bunch. A small, stilted affair overlooking the river and the pontoon bridge. It's a wooden café from where you can sit and watch the world go by.

Hon Chong *p104*

Relax Bar. Traveller friendly shack on the beach offering food, drinks, information and transfer to Phu Quoc.

🎵 Bars and clubs

Chau Doc *p97, map p97*

Victoria Chau Doc, see Sleeping, above, has a bar and a pool table.

✺ Festivals and events

Chau Doc *p97, map p97*

On all almost every weekend there is one festival or another. The busiest festivals are centred on **Tet**, 4 months after Tet and the mid-autumn **moon festival**.

Long Xuyen *p99*

20 Aug There are big celebrations on the birthday of Ton Duc Thang.

Rach Gia *p100*

Apart from the main festival they have occasional processions to thank Ca Ong, the God of the Sea, for protecting them.

▲ Activities and tours

Chau Doc *p97, map p97*
Swimming
There is a swimming pool at the Victoria
Chau Doc.

Therapies
A massage and fitness centre can be found
at the Victoria Chau Doc. All the services are
available to the general public.

Tour operators
Chau Doc Tourist Pier, next to the Victoria
hotel, T76-355 0949, btdlcd@vnn.vn. Offers
slow boat tours for US$10 per person or
speedboat tours for US$50 per person in
the area.
Delta Adventure Co, 55 Bis Le Loi St, T76-
355 0838, www.kimtravel.com. Organizes
speedboats to Phnom Penh and runs a
floating hotel. You might even be able to
book a local tour if you can find someone
behind reception that speaks English.
Mekong Tours, Vinh Phuoc Hotel, and at
14 Nguyen Huu Canh St, T76-386 8222, and
at the Thanh Nam 2 hotel where they are
particularly helpful, www.mekongtours.net.
Local trips include the fish farms, floating
markets and Cham village. Organizes delta
trips, city tours, Mekong homestays, trips to
Phu Quoc and boat trips to Phnom Penh
(US$10, departs 0700, 8-10 hrs or express boat,
US$25, departs 0800, 5 hrs; Cambodian visas
can be bought at the border). A/c and public
buses also booked; air ticketing; Open Bus
ticketing (to Can Tho hourly , US$5, 3 hrs; to Ha
Tien, US$7, 3 hrs; to HCMC hourly, US$9, 6 hrs);
and visa applications. Onward bus transport
to Can Tho and HCMC can include tour stops
on the way (from US$16-37). You need to
ask exactly what your payment includes
and whether any accommodation included
is individual or shared. Private express boat
transfer to My Tho, US$450; slow boat to Can
Tho, 4½ hrs, US$180, 6 people maximum.
Victoria Chau Doc, 32 Le Loi St, T76-386
5010, www.victoriahotels-asia.com. Tours
to Nui Sam, the city and a very interesting
tour to the floating market, fish farms and
Muslim village, cooking class, Tra Su forest
tour, farming tour and Le Jarai cruise tour.
Minimum 2 people for all tours.

Long Xuyen *p99*
Tour operators
See An Giang Tourimex, page 100.

Rach Gia *p100*
Tour operators
Kien Giang Travel Co, 5 Le Loi St, T77-386
7687. Mon-Fri 0700-1100, 1300-1500. Sat
0700-1100.
Kiengiang Tourist Public Company, 11
Ly Tu Trong St, T77-396 2024. Professional
and helpful and a smarter outfit than the
government-run Kien Giang Travel. More
English spoken too. Offers tours to Ha Tien
and Phu Quoc.

Ha Tien *p102, map p103*
Ha Tien Tourism Coop Ltd, 1 Phuong
Thanh St, T77-395 9598, hatientourism@
gmail.com. Organizes boat tickets to Phu
Quoc for US$9 and US$10. Open Buses to
HCMC, US$10 at 0900, 1130, 2200. Also to
Can Tho, Chau Doc, Vinh Long, My Tho and
Rach Gia. 3-day Mekong tours ending in
HCMC offered from US$55. Organizes buses
to Cambodia at 1200 and 1600: to Kep,
US$12; to Kampot US$15; to Sihanoukville,
US$20; to Phnom Penh at 1200 and 0600,
US$18. Cambodian visa organized, US$25.
These trips do not involve a change of bus.
Vietnam visa extensions also organized.

⊖ Transport

Chau Doc *p97, map p97*
Bicycle and motorbike
Mekong Tours rents bikes for US$2 a day
and motorbikes for US$10.

Boat
There are daily departures to **Phnom Penh**.
A couple of tour operators in town organize

boat tickets, see Tour operators, above.
Victoria Hotel speedboats go to Phnom Penh. Boats for hotel guests depart for Phnom Penh at 0700, returning 1330, US$100.

Make sure you have a valid Vietnamese visa if you are entering the country as these cannot be issued at the border crossing; Cambodian visas can be bought at all the nearby crossings. For other Cambodian border crossings, see page 99.

Bus
The new station is 3 km south from the town centre T76-386 7171. No English is spoken at the ticket office. Minibuses stop in town on Quang Trung St. Connections with **HCMC** (6 hrs), hourly, 0600-2400, 75,000d; **Tra Vinh**, 62,000d; **Ca Mau**, 81,000d; **Long Xuyen** (1½ hrs), 18,000d; **Can Tho**, every 30 mins, 0400-1700, 44,000d; **Rach Gia**, 38,000d; and **Ha Tien** (from 0600, every 3 hrs, 4 hrs, US$5) and other destinations in the delta. A *xe-ôm* from town is 15,000-20,000d.

There is an uncomfortable 10-hr bus ride from Chau Doc to **Phnom Penh** via **Moc Bai**, see page 99.

Mekong Tours, see Tour operators, runs a bus to **Phnom Penh** via **Tinh Bien** (see border crossings to Cambodia, page 99) at 0815, 5 hrs, US$25 with no change of bus.

See also under Tour operators for domestic and international bus transport.

Long Xuyen *p99*
Bus
The station is 1.5 km east of town at 414 Tran Hung Dao St. Minibuses stop on Hung Vuong St, not far from the cathedral. There are regular connections with **HCMC** (6-7 hrs), **Chau Doc** (1½ hrs), **Can Tho**, **Vinh Long** and other destinations in the delta. Some private minibus companies offer a faster and more comfortable service than the regular buses.

Car
The most direct route to Long Xuyen from **HCMC** is to cross the My Thuan Bridge near

Vinh Long. Alternatively, it's a pleasant drive on Highway 91 from **Can Tho** via O Mon. It is also possible to get here from **Cao Lanh** by taking 2 small ferries. For those who know the way, this is possibly the quickest and certainly the most scenic route back to HCMC.

Rach Gia *p100*
Air
Daily connections with **Phu Quoc Island**, 40 mins, and **HCMC**, 50 mins. The airport is at Rach Soi about 10 km south of Rach Gia. *Xe ôm* from the airport, 50,000d; taxi 80,000d.

Airline offices Vietnam Airlines, 16 Nguyen Trung Truc St, T77-392 4320.

Boat
Daily connections to **Phu Quoc**, departing from the ferry terminal on Nguyen Cong Tru St. A variety of ferry companies including **Superdong ferries**, T77-387 7742, **Duong Dong Express**, T77-387 9765, www.duongdongexpress.com.vn, and **Savanna** leave daily at 0745-0800 arriving 1030 and 1300, 270,000d, 200,000d for children. The ferries no longer arrive at An Thoi in the southern part of the island.

From the **Rach Meo** ferry terminal, 2 km south of town on Ngo Quyen St close to the junction with Nguyen Van Cu St, boats go to **Vinh Thuan** and **Ca Mau**, 0800, 100,000d. Travellers have reported overcrowding on the ferries, others have reported unlicensed boats in and out of Phu Quoc; highly dangerous.

Bus
There are 2 stations; the city centre terminal at Nguyen Binh Kiem St and a terminal at Rach Soi, 7 km south of town near the airport. From the 1st bus station, connections to **HCMC**, 8 hrs, **Can Tho**, **Vinh Long**, **Ha Tien** and **Long Xuyen**. Mai Linh and Phung Trang companies operate express buses to **HCMC**, 5 hrs, 115,000d. From the 2nd bus station, services to **Chau Doc** and **HCMC**.

Taxi

Mai Linh wait at the Nguyen Truc Trac city park. **Taxi Phuong Trinh**, 26 Nguyen Van Troi St, T77-387 8787.

Ha Tien *p102, map p103*
Bicycle

Ha Tien Tourism Coop Ltd rents bikes for 50,000d a day and motorbikes for 150,000d.

Boat

The ferry wharf is opposite the **Ha Tien hotel**. Ferries to **Phu Quoc** leave at 0800-0830 (120,000d) and at 1000, 100,000d. Note that the 1000 service arrives at **Nam Ninh** where there are few public transport options.

Bus

The bus station is on the way to the Cambodia border on Highyway 80 north of town. There are buses to **HCMC**, at 0700, 0800 and 0900, 10-12 hrs, 100,000d; and connections with **Rach Gia**, 4 hrs, 38,000d; **Chau Doc**, 52,000d; **Can Tho**, 83,000d; as well as other Delta towns. Reliable **Mai Linh** runs to **Rach Gia**, 45,000d. *Footprint* has news of scams involving illegally operated buses running out of Ha Tien and the Cambodia border. Make sure you buy a ticket at the real Ha Tien bus station. All real buses provide tickets in Vietnam. (Phong Ve means ticket office in Vietnamese). Ha Tien bus station is new with a ticket office. *Xe ôms* wait outside. *Xe ôm* to the Cambodia border, 30,000d; into town, 10,000d.

The **Ha Tien Service Tourism Co** wil transfer to the border for US$10. See border crossings to Cambodia, page 99.

A new road 5 km outside Ha Tien takes you to Tinh Bien and on to Chau Doc, shortening the Ha Tien-Chau Doc route.

❶ Directory

Chau Doc *p97, map p97*
Banks Vietinbank, 68-70 Nguyen Huu Canh St with ATM. BIDV, 7-9 Nguyen Huu Canh St, has a Visa ATM. Vietcombank, 1 Hung Vuong St. **Hospitals** Located opposite the Victoria Chau Doc Hotel, 5 Le Loi St, T76-356 0851.
Internet Available in the post office and also in Victoria Chau Doc Hotel. Fast connection at Internet, 30 Nguyen Huu Canh St. **Post office** 73 Le Loi St, open 0700-2000.

Long Xuyen *p99*
Banks Vietcombank, 1 Hung Vuong St (at the junction of Hung Vuong and Nguyen Thi Minh Khai St). **Hospitals** 2 Le Loi, T76-385 2989. **Internet** There are plenty of internet cafés, many of which are dotted along Hung Vuong St. **Post office** The main post office is at 106 Tran Hung Dao St (quite a way over the Hoang Dieu Bridge).

Rach Gia *p100*
Banks Sacombank, 37 Nguyen Hung Son St with ATM. There are ATMs and banks around the city. **Hospitals** 46 Le Loi, T77-386 3328. **Internet** Apart from the post office there is a selection along Nguyen Trung Truc St and at 72 Nguyen Van Troi St. **Post office** 1 Duong Mau Than St, T77-386 2551. Internet and 171 international dialling services.

Ha Tien *p102, map p103*
Banks Agribank is located on 37 Lam Son St on the corner of Phung Thanh St with a currency exchange and ATM. Sacombank, 16 Tran Hau St; ATM. **Hospitals** On the corner of Mac Cuu and Bach Dang Sts, T77-385 2666. **Internet** In the main post office and at Ha Tien Tourism. **Post office** 3 To Chau St, T77-385 2182.

Phu Quoc Island

Phu Quoc is Vietnam's largest island, lying off the southwest coast of Vietnam. The island remains largely undeveloped with beautiful sandy beaches along much of its coastline and forested hills inland. Most of the beaches benefit from crystal-clear waters making it perfect for swimming and a place well worth visiting for those with some time to spend in southern Vietnam. The island's remoteness and lack of infrastructure has meant that it is only recently that tourism has started developing and the pace of development has been slower than in other parts of the country owing to the lack of power and water supplies to much of the island.

However, Phu Quoc is set to expand at a phenomenal rate as multi-million dollar projects have been given the green light The island's status as a remote, undeveloped bolt hole, is over. Phu Quoc's northernmost tip lies just outside Cambodian territorial waters and, like other parts of present-day Vietnam in this area, it has been fought over, claimed and reclaimed by Thai, Khmer and Viet. At the moment some of the island is reserved for military use and hence certain areas are restricted but, despite this, there remains plenty to explore. ▸ *For listings, see pages 113-116.*

Ins and outs

Getting there You can get to Phu Quoc by boat from Rach Gia or Ha Tien or by plane from Rach Gia and Ho Chi Minh City. Most hotels will provide a free pick-up service from the airport if accommodation is booked in advance. The same does not apply to transfers from the ferry port. *Xe ôm* drivers meet the ferries. ▸ *See Transport, page 116.*

Getting around While some of the island's roads are surfaced many are still dirt tracks and so the best way to get around the entire island is by motorbike (see Transport, page 116), although this could prove desperately hot and dusty. There are plenty of motorbike taxis and motorbikes are easily available and cheap to hire. The only problem that visitors are likely to encounter is the very limited signposting which can make some places pretty hard to find without some form of local assistance. Cars with drivers at fairly reasonable costs are available. Ask at hotels.

Tourist information Most of the resorts are very happy to arrange tours and they are a good source of up-to-date information. There are several tour operators which will provide plenty of information, see Tour operators.

History

Historically, the island is renowned for its small part in the triumph of the Nguyen Dynasty. In 1765 Pigneau de Behaine was sent here as a young seminarist to train Roman Catholic missionaries; by chance he was on the island when Nguyen Anh (son of emperor-to-be Gia Long) arrived, fleeing the Tay Son. Pigneau's role in the rise of the Nguyen Dynasty is described on page 191. Another link between the island and Vietnamese history is that it was here, in 1919, that the civil servant Ngo Van Chieu communed with the spirit world and made contact with the Supreme Being, leading to the establishment of the Cao Dai religion.

Around the island

Duong Dong is the main town on the island and many of the hotels and resorts are near here on Truong Beach. Millions of fish can be seen laid out to dry on land and on tables – all destined for the pot. Before being bottled they are fermented. At the Khai Hoan **fish sauce factory** ① *free*, huge barrels act as vats, each containing fish and salt. If the sauce is made in concrete vats, the taste is lost and so the sauce is cheaper.

The **Coi Nguon Museum** ① *149 Tran Hung Dao St, T77-398 0206, www.coi nguonphuquoc.com, daily 0700-1700, 1 English-speaking guide*, displays a huge amount of island creatures, fishing paraphernalia, old currency and Chinese ceramics from shipwrecked boats. The guide could not explain, however, how a private collector has amassed such a large haul of natural and man-made treasures.

About 10 km south of Dong Duong is the **Phu Quoc Pearl Gallery** ① *T91-399 3202, 0800-1800*. Just offshore 10,000 South Sea pearls are collected each year. A video demonstrates the farming operation and the tasting of pearl meat and the pearl process is illustrated in the gallery. Jewellery is for sale. Some 100 m south of the pearl farm on the coastal road there are two **whale dedication temples**, Lang Ca Ong. In front of one is a crude whale/dolphin statue.

Ganh Dau, at the northwest tip, is 35 km from Duong Dong. The townsfolk speak Khmer because refugees escaping the Khmer Rouge came here and settled with the locals. The Cambodian coast is 4-5 km away and can be seen, as can the last island

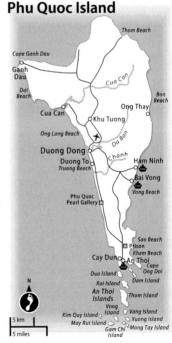

Phu Quoc Island

Thom Beach
Cape Ganh Dau
Ganh Dau
Cua Can
Dai Beach
Bon Beach
Cua Can
Ong Thay
Khu Tuong
Ong Lang Beach
Da Ban
Duong Dong
Duong To
Truong Beach
Chanh
Ham Ninh
Bai Vong
Vong Beach
Phu Quoc Pearl Gallery
Sao Beach
Prison
Khem Beach
Cay Dun
An Thoi
Cape Ong Doi
N
Dua Island
Dam Island
Roi Island
An Thoi Islands
Thom Island
5 km
Vong Island
Vang Island
5 miles
Kim Quy Island
Xuong Island
May Rut Island
Mong Tay Island
Gam Chi Island

of Vietnam. (The Cambodians actually claim Phu Quoc as their own). The beach has a few palms and rocks to clamber on and there is a restaurant. **Dai Beach**, south of Ganh Danh, is a strip of white sand backed by casuarinas overlooking Turtle Island. The water is clear but there are no facilities. Inland from here the area is heavily forested but the wood is protected by law. In this part of the island fish are laid out to dry on large trestle-tables or on the ground for use as fertilizer. South of Dai Beach is **Ong Lang Beach** where there are a couple of resorts, see Sleeping.

The dazzling white sands of **Sao Beach** on the southeast coast are stunning and worth visiting by motorbike. There are a couple of restaurants at the back of the beach.

The inland streams and waterfalls (**Da Ban** and **Chanh** streams) are not very dramatic in the dry season but still provide a relaxing place to swim and walk in the forests.

One of the biggest draws are the boat trips around the **An Thoi islands**, scattered islands, like chips off a block, off the southern coast, which offer opportunities for swimming, snorkelling, diving and fishing. It is also possible to stop off to visit an interesting fishing village at **Thom Island**.

Phu Quoc Island listings

For Sleeping and Eating price codes and other relevant information, see pages 10-13.

Sleeping

During peak periods such as Christmas and Tet it is advisable to book accommodation well in advance. Representatives from different resorts meet flights, providing free transfers and touting for business. Most of the resorts lie along the west coast on Long Beach to the south of Duong Dong and are within a few kilometres of the airport. Others are on On Lang Beach.

$$$$ Cassia Cottage, T77-384 8395, Long Beach, www.cassiacottage.com. A small resort set in front of a small length of beach and focused around a pool. Families will love the inflatable water toys collection. Cooking classes and volleyball are offered for the active. Rooms (with no TV) are lovely with bathrooms. Diners can eat in the garden.

$$$$ Chen La Resort & Spa, Ong Lang Beach, T77-399 5895, www.chenla-resort. com. A very inviting resort with lovely villas set back from the white-sand beach with alfresco bathrooms. Smaller-roomed semi-detached bungalows face the sea. The golden sands are dotted with umbrellas, and there's an infinity pool, spa, watersports and

atmospheric restaurant.
$$$$ La Veranda, Tran Hung Dao St, Long Beach, T77-398 2988, www.laverandaresort. com. A beautiful luxury resort with rooms and villas set in luscious gardens leading on to the main beach on the island. All rooms are beautifully furnished and come with TVs, DVD players and wireless internet. Deluxe rooms and villas come with gorgeous 4-poster beds and drapes. There's a spa, pool and the delicious food of the **Peppertree Restaurant**. The service is exceptional.
$$$$-$$$ Mango Bay, Ong Lang Beach, T90-338 2207, www.mangobayphuquoc. com. A small and exclusive environmentally friendly private resort in tropical gardens located on the beach close to pepper farms. A perfect spot. Bungalows are made from rammed earth and come with fans and coconut doorknobs and are kitted out with bamboo furniture and tiled floors. There are also fishermen's huts and rooms, with a wonderful, large communal veranda. Some have outdoor bathrooms in bamboo-enclosed patios which are very attractive. The restaurant provides a mixture of Vietnamese and Western food at reasonable prices. Price includes breakfast.
$$$$-$$$ Saigon Phu Quoc Resort, 1 Trang Hung Dao St, Long Beach, T77-384

6999, www.vietnamphuquoc.com. Well-finished a/c bungalows set on a hillside garden overlooking the sea. The resort has good facilities including a decent pool, tennis court, internet access and a reasonably priced restaurant serving international food.

$$$ Mai House Resort, Long Beach, T77-384 7003, maihouseresort@yahoo.com. This is a really lovely resort run by Tuyet Mai and Gerard Bezardin set in large gardens in front of a slice of beach. The 20 bungalows feature 4-poster beds, bathrooms and balconies. Sea-view rooms are bigger. The restaurant (with Wi-Fi access) overlooks the beach.

$$$ Tropicana Resort, Long Beach, T77-384 7127, tropicana_vn@yahoo.com. The resort has high-quality wooden bungalows set in a tropical garden next to the beach with a pool but some of the bungalows and the garden are looking unloved compared to the gardens of neighbouring resorts; they've even neglected to put a sign up to the resort on the main road. Prices vary according to facilities although the beachfront balconied bungalows are overpriced. The resort has one of the best restaurants, a well-stocked bar and internet access.

$$$-$$ Bo Resort, Ong Lang Beach, T77-986 142/3, www.boresort.com. This feels like a great escape with 18 stilted bungalows set on a hillside amid flourishing gardens. Rooms come with large rustic bathrooms and alfresco showers. There's no road access to the wild stretch of beach where there are pines, hammocks, kayaks and a beach bar. There's Wi-Fi in the restaurant/bar and candlelight at night. The owners are warm and friendly.

$$$-$$ Kim Hoa Resort, 88/2 Tran Hung Dao St, Long Beach, T77-384 7039, www.kimhoaresort.com. This resort that has expanded to offer 72 rooms: typical wooden bungalows are right on a strip of sand in front of the resort as well as garden rooms, pool view rooms and rooms in a block away from the beach; these are the cheapest. One of the oldest resorts on the island.

$$$-$$ Sao Bien, Tran Hung Dao St, Long Beach, T77-398 2161, www.seastarresort.com. Spacious but spartan rooms at this resort with 38 bungalows of mixed price and a long stretch of beach. Garden rooms at the rear of the property are cheaper than those nearer the beachfront. Cheapest are those in a hotel block. Wi-Fi at reception and restaurant only.

$$$-$$ Thien Hai Son, 68 Tran Hung Dao St, Long Beach, T77-398 3044, www.phuquocthienhaison.com. This is a pleasant resort with comfortable rooms but characterless. There's only a thin strip of beach out front. A last resort if nicer properties are booked up.

$$ Freedomland, Ong Lang Beach, 10 mins' walk from beach, T77-399 4891, www.freedomlandphuquoc.com. Run by Peter, this resort creates a community vibe as all guests eat together at the large dinner table. Bungalows are scattered around the grounds. 4 of the rooms have private bathroom and 4 share. Boat and motos can be rented.

$$-$ Beach Club, Long Beach, T77-398 0998, www.beachclubvietnam.com. Luscious golden sands and thatched beach umbrellas at this small resort, the furthest from the town and thus not conveniently located. If you don't want to leave the resort and kick back for a while this is perfect. If you want more activity, choose a resort closer to town. The 6 rooms and 4 bungalows are all close to the sea. It's good value and so always booked up. Reserve well in advance.

$$-$ Thang Loi, Ong Lang Beach, T77-398 5002, www.phuquoc.de. Wooden bungalows with fans, set in a remote coconut plantation north of Duong Dong. It has a good bar and restaurant with friendly German owners. There is a library, music and great food including *weiner schnitzel*. A jetty has been built out over the sea. Closed May-Sep. Breakfast not included.

$ Kim Phung, Tran Hung Dao St, Duong Dong, T77-398 1727. This is a basic but clean town hotel with rooms in a little courtyard out back. It would be fine and convenient for those with no budget for a resort break. It's on the main strip amid the restaurants and dive operators.

Eating

The food on Phu Quoc is generally very good, especially the fish and seafood. On the street in Duong Dong try the delicious *gio cuong* (fresh spring rolls) but do be aware that some of the market stalls appear to cook using water taken straight from the river.

Most of the resorts mentioned have beachfront restaurants.

Ocean Bar & Grill & Winestore, 60 Tran Hung Dao St, T77-399 4268, winestore.pq@gmail.com. The owner of this place gives the biggest welcome in Phu Quoc. Friendly ambience, tasty and varied Vietnamese and pan-Asian dishes and a great view of the sunset for an early dinner.

Pepper's, 89 Tran Hung Dao St, T77-384 8773. A popular Italian restaurant set away from the beach. Service is a bit slack though.

Buddy's, 26 Nguyen Trai St, T77-399 4181. Western-style café with roadside view serving up ice cream at 20,000d per scoop.

German B, 5 Tran Hung Dao St. A conveniently located German bakery and café on the main road. Service is friendly and efficient.

La Craft & Cafe, 11 Tran Hung Dao St, T90-820 1102. A tiny streetside caff serving yoghurts, shakes and breakfasts on cute black-lacquered furniture under beige umbrellas. It's opposite the market entrance.

My Lan, Sao Beach, T77-384 4447, dungmyt@yahoo.com. Daily 0600-2100. A gorgeous setting on a gorgeous beach. Tables are under thatched roofs. Sit back and enjoy a beer with fresh seafood dishes.

Bars and clubs

The Dog Bar, 88 Tran Hung Dao St, near the Thien Hai Son Resort, T90-381 4688. Well-located beer den with cold drinks, pool and sports TV.

Shopping

If you have Vietnamese friends or family and return without a bottle of the fish sauce you will be in trouble. However, you cannot take the sauce on a **Vietnam Airlines** flight.

Apart from the fish sauce there is a surprisingly good choice of goods to buy. Do remember, however, that no matter how pretty the coral ornaments and ashtrays may look, they are cut from living coral.

Activities and tours

Watersports are available at the hotels. Also cycling tours, boat tours and walking.

Diving
Rainbow Divers, Tran Hung Dao St, close to the market, T91-723 9433 (mob), www.divevietnam.com Long-standing operation with a very good reputation.

Tour operators
Discovery Tour, 32 Tran Hung Dao St, Duong Dong T77-384 6587, www.phuquoctravel.com.vn. Daily 0700-1800.

Ha Tien Tourism Coop Ltd, 37A Tran Hung Dao St, Duong Dong, T77-398 2888, hatientourism@gmail.com. Branch office of the one in Ha Tien that is run by the on-the-ball and helpful Marie. Sells boat tickets and has free internet for customers.

John's Tours, New Star Café, 143 Tran Hung Dao St, T91-910 7086, www.johnislandtours.com. Run by John Tran out of the **New Star Café** (next to the alley to **La Veranda**) and various kiosks on the beach as well as hotel desks. Snorkelling, squid fishing, island tours and car hire can be arranged. Prices from US$15. Car hire with driver also arranged.

Tony Travel, 100 Tran Hung Dao St or based at the **Rainbow Divers** office on Tran Hung Dao St opposite the market, T913-197334, tonytravelpq@yahoo.com.vn. Kiosks on the beach too. Tony speaks fluent English. In his stable are island tours, snorkelling to the south and north islands, deep-sea fishing excursions, car and motorbike rental and hotel and transport reservations. Prices from US$15. Snorkelling tours make sure you're fitted with a mask and snorkel properly.

⊖ Transport

Air
There are daily flights to **HCMC** and **Rach Gia**.
Airline offices Vietnam Airlines, 122 Nguyen Trung Truc St, Duong Dong, T77-399667.

Boat
Ferries leave from Bai Vong port in the southeastern part of the island and Ham Ninh in the east. An Thoi port in the south is closed for renovation. See also Getting there, page 111, for details.
Superdong, 1 Tran Hung Dao St, Duong Dong, T77-348 6180, to **Rach Gia** from Bai Vong at 1300 arriving 1535. 270,000d.
Duong Dong Express, www.duongdong express.com.vn, leaves for **Rach Gia** at 1245 arriving 1515, 270,000d; children 200,000d.
Savanna, 36 Tran Hung Dao St, T77-399 2999, at Bai Vong, T77-399 2555. Leaves at 1305 arriving **Rach Gia** at 1535, 270,000d.
Vinashin, 21 Nguyen Trai St, T77-260 0155, leaves 0810.
Cawaco from Ham Ninh to Ha Tien at 0830 arriving 1000, 160,000d. Also departs Bai Vong 1400 arriving 1520. Bus picks up from agents, at 1200, 20,000d, for the **Bai Vong** departure. No public transport to Ham Ninh; taxi 160,000d.

Cars, bicycles and motorbikes
Cars, motorbikes and bicycles can be rented from resorts.

Taxis
Mai Linh, No 10 30 Thang 4 St, Duong Dong, T77-397 9797.
Sasco, 379 Nguyen Trung Truc St, T77-399 5599. Taxis from the airport to Ong Lang are around US$15 and from the port, US$8.

⊕ Directory

Banks Agribank, 2 Tran Hung Dao St, Duong Dong, also cashes TCs; ATM. **Phu Quoc Bank**, Duong Dong, cashes TCs. **Vietcombank**, 0700-1100, 1300-1700, has Visa and MasterCard ATM. **Hospitals** The hospital is in Khu Pho, 1 Duong Dong, T77-384 8075. **Internet** Available at resorts; some have Wi-Fi. Terminals at **John's Tours**, New Star Café, 143 Tran Hung Dao St.
Post office Phu Quoc Post Office, 2 Tran Hung Dao St Duong Dong, 0645-2030.

Contents

Footnotes

Index

Titles available in the Footprint *Focus* range

Latin America	UK RRP	US RRP
Bahia & Salvador	£7.99	$11.95
Buenos Aires & Pampas	£7.99	$11.95
Costa Rica	£8.99	$12.95
Cuzco, La Paz & Lake Titicaca	£8.99	$12.95
El Salvador	£5.99	$8.95
Guadalajara & Pacific Coast	£6.99	$9.95
Guatemala	£8.99	$12.95
Guyana, Guyane & Suriname	£5.99	$8.95
Havana	£6.99	$9.95
Honduras	£7.99	$11.95
Nicaragua	£7.99	$11.95
Paraguay	£5.99	$8.95
Quito & Galápagos Islands	£7.99	$11.95
Recife & Northeast Brazil	£7.99	$11.95
Rio de Janeiro	£8.99	$12.95
São Paulo	£5.99	$8.95
Uruguay	£6.99	$9.95
Venezuela	£8.99	$12.95
Yucatán Peninsula	£6.99	$9.95

Asia	UK RRP	US RRP
Angkor Wat	£5.99	$8.95
Bali & Lombok	£8.99	$12.95
Chennai & Tamil Nadu	£8.99	$12.95
Chiang Mai & Northern Thailand	£7.99	$11.95
Goa	£6.99	$9.95
Hanoi & Northern Vietnam	£8.99	$12.95
Ho Chi Minh City & Mekong Delta	£7.99	$11.95
Java	£7.99	$11.95
Kerala	£7.99	$11.95
Kolkata & West Bengal	£5.99	$8.95
Mumbai & Gujarat	£8.99	$12.95

Africa	UK RRP	US RRP
Beirut	£6.99	$9.95
Damascus	£5.99	$8.95
Durban & KwaZulu Natal	£8.99	$12.95
Fès & Northern Morocco	£8.99	$12.95
Jerusalem	£8.99	$12.95
Johannesburg & Kruger National Park	£7.99	$11.95
Kenya's beaches	£8.99	$12.95
Kilimanjaro & Northern Tanzania	£8.99	$12.95
Zanzibar & Pemba	£7.99	$11.95

Europe	UK RRP	US RRP
Bilbao & Basque Region	£6.99	$9.95
Granada & Sierra Nevada	£6.99	$9.95
Málaga	£5.99	$8.95
Orkney & Shetland Islands	£5.99	$8.95
Skye & Outer Hebrides	£6.99	$9.95

North America	UK RRP	US RRP
Vancouver & Rockies	£8.99	$12.95

Australasia	UK RRP	US RRP
Brisbane & Queensland	£8.99	$12.95
Perth	£7.99	$11.95

For the latest books, e-books and smart phone app releases, and a wealth of travel information, visit us at: www.footprinttravelguides.com.

footprint travel guides.com

Join us on facebook for the latest travel news, product releases, offers and amazing competitions: www.facebook.com/footprintbooks.com.